Scree

Scree
Fred Wah

THE COLLECTED EARLIER POEMS, 1962–1991

EDITED BY JEFF DERKSEN

Talonbooks

Talonbooks
278 East First Avenue, Vancouver, British Columbia, Canada V5T 1A6
www.talonbooks.com

First printing: 2015

Typeset in Garth Graphic
Printed and bound in Korea

Interior and cover design by Typesmith
On the cover:
Takao Tanabe
Envelope Sketch, 1967
serigraph ed., 10/50
SFU Art Collection. Purchase, 1967

Talonbooks acknowledges the financial support of the Canada Council for the Arts, the Government of Canada through the Canada Book Fund, and the Province of British Columbia through the British Columbia Arts Council and the Book Publishing Tax Credit.

LIBRARY AND ARCHIVES CANADA CATALOGUING IN PUBLICATION

Wah, Fred, 1939–
[Poems. Selections]
Scree : the collected earlier poems, 1962–1991 / Fred Wah ; edited by and with an introduction by Jeff Derksen.

Includes index.
ISBN 978-0-88922-947-1 (BOUND).—ISBN 978-0-88922-948-8 (PAPERBACK)

I. Derksen, Jeff, 1958–, editor II. Title.

PS8545.A28A6 2015 C811'.54 C2015-904279-8

Contents

Mountain (1967)

Tree (1972)

from Among (1972)

Earth (1974)

Pictograms from the Interior of B.C. (1975)

Owners Manual (1981)

from Loki Is Buried at Smoky Creek (1980)

Rooftops (1988)

from So Far (1991)

Breathin' My Name with a Sigh (1981)

474 Breathe dust like you breathe wind…

476 my father hurt-

477 Poem lightens the lungs Diana says meaning

478 have to do

479 WHAT'S IT LIKE TO HOLD YOURSELF IN

480 WANT RIVER PIECE OUT OF THIS MOVING RIVER
TREES BANK

481 IN THE ARMS OF THE FAMILY

482 now you're not thirteen

483 all over

484 when I will be water

485 Loki is buried at Smoky Creek

486 Loki warned me

487 your name is my name

488 Fish under yourself (self)

489 just counted for his death I

490 try it adds up to a colour

491 "got" his eyes, sister

492 breathing in the water so much a breath

493 Sigh.   a relief of muscles and blood flowing

494 The diaphragm of the clouds…

495 Sigh. A tenuous slight stream of air escapes…

496 When he wanted to stay alive but was drowning…

497 to travel south

498 rivers breathe water

499 Father it is fall

500 the gap

501 for / I forgot

502 to get it how the river in its mud flows downstream…

503 the father grandfather

504 baseball (the)

505 runs the cycle

506 FORTY-FIRST THE YEAR THE STREET …

507 World / house open to the music

508 Once / made it

509 A hight

510 when you die it snows

511 Breathless / news

512 swimming for dying

513 trumpet / grammar

514 waiting for Saskatchewan

515 One more thing

517 I / jazz

518 next spring

Grasp the Sparrow's Tail (1982)

from Waiting for Saskatchewan (1985)

ELITE

THIS DENDRITE MAP: FATHER/MOTHER HAIBUN

Reader's Manual

An Introduction to the Poetics and Contexts of Fred Wah's Early Poetry

A geographical term for a splay of small rocks that have been cracked free of a mountainside through the long-term action of freezing and thawing, *scree* indicates both the accumulation of angular rocks and the triangular fan down the mountain or hill. As a title for this collection of Fred Wah's poetry from 1962 to 1991, *scree* is fitting because it is a deceptively simple word that wavers between an image of a mountainside and pure sound. Etymologically derived from the Old Norse term for "landslide" through to the Old English term for "glide," *scree* is linked to movement and process. Wah's poetry, particularly the poetry from the thirteen books gathered in this volume, is distinguished by its attention to the movement of language, the dynamism of poetic form, and a sense of place itself understood as a process of movement and stasis. As Susan Rudy proposes, *scree* then becomes an apt metaphor for Wah's poetry as a whole: "For Wah, writing gives and slides" ("Fred Wah – Among," 7). George Bowering, in his perceptive introduction to Wah's selected works volume from 1980, *Loki Is Buried at Smoky Creek*, suggests, "It [*scree*] makes a good concrete image for evidence that all things of the earth, even mountains, are moving & changing" (19). Bowering identifies *scree* as a particular image of the interior of British Columbia, where much of Wah's early work is grounded, as well as pointing to the complexities of landscape and the engagement with nature in Wah's poetry.

Scree is also the name of a magazine that Wah edited, produced on a Gestetner mimeograph machine, from his South Slocan home in the Kootenay region of British Columbia, in the early 1970s, where he returned to work at Selkirk College after studying with two of the most influential and enduring figures of New American Poetry, Robert Creeley (at the University of New Mexico) and Charles Olson (at SUNY – Buffalo). Previously, Wah had edited *SUM* (out of Albuquerque) and, during his undergraduate days in the early 1960s at the University of British Columbia, had been a founding editor of *Tish: A Poetry Newsletter*, a magazine that opened an axis within Canadian poetry to the emergent poets and little magazines of the United States while also investigating place, space, and the local in relation to speech, images, and history. This process-based poetry radically opened the shape of poetry to come in Canada by its experimentations with Creeley's proposition (derived from Charles Olson) that "form is never more than an extension of content." Wah, and the core *Tish* poets – who include Daphne Marlatt, George Bowering, Frank Davey, Lionel Kearns, Jamie Reid, Maria (Gladys) Hindmarch, and Robert Hogg – cut across the grain of Canadian literature in the 1960s and surprisingly shook up the terrain of literary production in Canada with their modest, stapled newsletter.

Wah, and the generation of writers who emerged in the early 1960s, began writing and publishing at a time when both the cultural project of Canadian literature and a national identity were being shaped as part of Canada's belated modernist project. Canada, the narrative goes, was seeking to step out of the shadows of Britain, to distinguish itself from the superpower to the south, and to take position as a modern nation within a postwar world system. Within this frame of cultural nationalism, as Louis Cabri indicates, "The idea of *Tish* would stir up controversy even though Fred Wah and other poets associated with *Tish* ... were articulating Canada's western cultural geography in their writing and even though most of Canadian verse was still largely beholden to British paradigms of poetic form"(ix). And, as Cabri goes on to point out, *Tish* was the extension of a project within Canadian literature rather than a dramatic avant-gardist break: "The *Tish* poets picked up where poet-editors Louis Dudek in Montreal and Raymond Souster left off – continuing the turn away from British paradigms of rhythm, rhyme, reason, toward free-verse American paradigms" (ibid). *Tish* strengthened this north-south influence, picking up on the questioning of form and materiality that moved through art, music, and literature, and brought innovation in free jazz, the emergence of Conceptual art, and the fraying of literary modernism and the shift to postmodernist approaches.

Against this backdrop of social and cultural transformation, there was a push for this national cultural project to take shape as Canada rushed into its centenary in 1967, crowned by its grand world exposition in cosmopolitan Montreal, Expo 67. Yet, as historian Bryan D. Palmer argues, "No sooner had this national identity emerged from its tortured past than it imploded as new challenges and new discontentments littered the landscape and clouded the horizons of being Canadian. The 'things' of national identity were, by 1968, clearly falling apart" (420). Palmer turns up the heat to provocatively argue that the 1960s in Canada, "brought down decisively what needed dismantling, but could not, having accomplished this, build the kind of alternative that was required" (429). Yet, from a cultural perspective, this "falling apart" opened up the fissures and spaces that Wah and other writers have both flourished in and prised even further as the literary terrain of Canada was challenged and redefined beyond the 1960s and into the 1970s and 1980s. Roy Miki, whose own work helped develop this transformation, narrates this long process: "The 1970s and early 1980s, especially in large urban centres, saw the emergence of alternative groups, variously self-identified, whose 'voices' resisted and often refused the dominant cultural forms of the Canadian nation by making visible the covered-over or elided histories in the nation's past. Soon we were no longer in search of 'a' or 'the' Canadian identity, the predominant social quest of the 1960s" ("Global Drift," 149). Wah succinctly describes the transformation of this cultural quest of a national unity to a productive resistance that produced difference within and against an imagined national coherence: "The tactical imagination of 'national unity' is, for some writers, a 'disunity' (*Faking It*, 67).[1] The productive irony, for Wah and other writers, is that disunity has also been an extremely productive space and a tactical imagination for poetry.

However, a mapping of Canadian literature from the 1960s through the 1980s cannot be one of a move from a brief unity, willed together through Canada's cultural institutions with the state's backing, to a fragmented disunity that emerged after official multiculturalism and the challenges to it from minority writers, racialized writers, queer writers, Indigenous authors, and writers who continue to write in the shadow of the imagination of the national culture. These writers brought knowledges, histories, forms, and distinct voices into Canadian literature at the very moment it was being drawn more strongly into a globalization of culture that refigured national cultures rather than eroded them. Kit Dobson proposes this as a transnational narrative in which "the nationalism of the 1960s and '70s that worked to consolidate this literature, and the multiculturalisms of the '80s and '90s, and the new millennium that have sought to reconsolidate it through dismantling its ethnocentrism, have become conjoined with the world of globalization" (x). Another reading could configure Canadian literature as always being globalized and differentiated in various ways, and that the emergence of "discontentments" to the national project uncovered difference, internationalism, and globality within Canadian literature. Reading the works in *Scree* today gives a sense of the questions, coherences, and fault lines within Canadian literature as well as the inevitable and powerful external influences, reconfigurations, and alignments that a cultural project springing out of a national imperative both encounter and counter.

Within this context, as Miki and Wah argue, the idea of a unified national literature, even as a contingent project, can never be universal, never be lived from sea to sea. Once the myth of unity was sprung or fell apart, Canadian literature has been marked by the continual production of difference that has reshaped, through critique and through alternative visions, what might be asked of a national literature in a globalized world. The cultural and social signposts along the way of the shift from this tenuous national identity, fabulously constructed out of historical exclusions, contingent inclusions, and denials of a colonial present (all of which provide the social and cultural history reflected in *Scree*) range from the development of official multiculturalism in Canada from a 1971 White Paper to a bill in 1988; the Indigenous movement from opposition to the White Paper on Indian Affairs that Jean Chrétien introduced in 1969 to the standoff at Oka between the Mohawk nation of Kanesatake, the Quebec provincial police, and the Canadian armed forces in 1990; and the Japanese Canadian Redress movement, begun in 1983 and signed as an agreement in 1988. Looming in the future was the watershed event of the 1994 Writing Thru Race conference in which the cultural hegemony tried to hold the illusions of a Canadian identity and literature and to block a "more complex understanding of the space of the nation" (Lai, 214) just at the moment when globalization as a cultural and economic process was intensifying – a process the state hastened through even as it had sat in uneasy conjunction with the unravelling of the national cultural narrative. Over this period of time, national literatures have thoroughly transformed from *instruments* of a cultural project to differentiated cultural products within a global context where the border between culture and the market has been blurred even as the actual border of nations has become sharply guarded. So, while the question of the 1960s might have been – What is Canadian literature? – today the question is more speculative and queries Why *Canadian* literature?

I paint this broader picture, or rescaling, of Canadian literature because Fred Wah's poetry, no matter how localized it is in the particulars of life, landscape, language, and perception, has also always been transnational and globalized; from the confluence of poetics across the Americas to Europe and Asia, to the content of the works themselves, with its configurations of a hybrid identity that fully develops through this volume (which leads to Wah's groundbreaking book that refigured writing that engaged with the politics of identity – rather than the rather narrowly defined "identity politics" – *Diamond Grill* [1996]). The great subtlety of the poetry in *Scree* is in its expansiveness: a movement from a grounded localness that carries a weight in its details of place and in its precision of language, to syntactically compressed narratives that sweep from "my mountains" of British Columbia to "your [Wah's father] China youth and the images of place for you before you were twenty are imbued with the green around Canton rice fields, humid Hong Kong masses" ("Elite 8," *Waiting for Saskatchewan*, 67–68). *Scree* pulls together the early and unsure *Tish* poems and thirteen books – *Lardeau* (1965), *Mountain* (1967), *Among* (1972), *Tree* (1972), *Earth* (1974), *Pictograms from the Interior of B.C.* (1975), *Loki Is Buried at Smoky Creek* (1980), *Breathin' My Name with a Sigh* (1981), *Owners Manual* (1981), *Grasp the Sparrow's Tail* (1982), *Waiting for Saskatchewan* (1985), *Rooftops* (1988), and *So Far* (1991) – and it does so in a manner that creates a movement that foregrounds the way in which themes and poetic forms (the relationship of form and content again!) are in dialogue throughout the book. After many readings of the gathered work, Fred and I decided to deviate from a chronology shaped by the book's publication dates and instead we ordered *Scree* roughly according to the dates the poems were written with a particular eye to the shifts and development of poetic form. The dialogue between Fred Wah's earlier works tests the possibilities of a poetics of place, of a syntactic dynamism opened by the North American postwar experiments in form and a push against the Western box of knowledge (a push that is threaded through 1960s counterculture up to the globalization of the early

1990s). The later works in *Scree* move away from the more open forms of the earlier works and combine Japanese poetic forms with the dense and materialistic use of language in order to approach the narratives of place, diaspora, and belonging that recur throughout the works in *Scree.* This relationship of the testing of poetic forms and the shifts, developments, and repetitions of themes cohere powerfully in "This Dendrite Map: Father/Mother Haibun" from the Governor General's Award–winning *Waiting for Saskatchewan* and sets the ground for *Diamond Grill.*

Within this trajectory, the intensity of memory, the revisiting of shared domestic moments tinged with a greater understanding of their emotional or affective impact, and vibrancy of language sprung free of the expectation of poetics and narrative syntax make *Breathin' My Name with a Sigh* a fulcrum within this collection. It is, as Wah writes in that collection's brief yet powerful preface, "a book of remembering": "Somehow a selection of the information of a life is made and placed in such a way as to not only make note of it but also to allow it to generate a truth otherwise impossible to locate." The relationship of formal variation and formal innovation in *Breathin' My Name with a Sigh* make this slender and minimally designed book a dynamic process that tries to "generate a truth otherwise impossible to locate" out of "a selection of information about a life," as Wah also writes in the preface. From this, *Breathin' My Name with a Sigh* becomes a collective biography – related to what Wah would later call a "biotext" – built from particular information and images. To foreground how *Breathin' My Name with a Sigh* is a catalyst for the poetics that more densely investigate the intersection of the transnational and the local and the national and the global, yet all packed into particulars of a life and of specific places, we have set it in relation with *Grasp the Sparrow's Tail* (printed in Kyoto, Japan, in 1982) and selections from *Waiting for Saskatchewan*. To do this, we split the works from the book *So Far* (which in itself was a selected works of serial and occasional poems published in 1991), placing the works in it from the early to mid-1980s before *Breathin' My Name with a Sigh* and anchoring the *utanikis* (a Japanese form that merges a diaristic entry with the haiku) from *So Far* (written between 1987 and 1989) at the end of the book.

Constructing the book in this manner has a poetics. This construction or ordering points to the ways in which the temporalities of writing are tied to the rhythms of a body as well as social rhythms – this joining is what the French philosopher of space, Henri Lefebvre, has called a rhythmanalysis. Using rhythmanalysis to read Wah's work illuminates how, as Lefebvre proposes, "Time and space, the cyclical and the linear, exert a reciprocal action" (8). Within the individual books and poems in *Scree*, there is often a non-linear sense of time that makes the repetitions of images and stories and the reworking of times, places, and memories so material and so affective. Constructing *Scree* as a book, we have applied rhythmanalysis to bring this relationship of time, place, history, and memory to the surface.

At the same time, each of Wah's books are built as books. The book is a unit of writing and the individual poems never fully exist on their own.

Scree, then, is a book of books – but a book on its own with attention to the movement from poem to poem and from book to book. To emphasize this insistence on the book as a composition and as a cultural object, we have reproduced both *Earth* and *Tree* in colour facsimile. The material aspects of their production – the coloured paper of *Earth* (which was within the series initiated by Charles Olson, "A Curriculum for the Soul") and the hand drawing and large type of *Tree* (the book was typed on an elementary school typewriter and printed at the Argenta Friends School at the north end of Kootenay Lake) – not only catch the technology of publishing at that time, but they bring the energetic design of 1970s poetry books – a period with an explosion of little magazines that defined the literary landscape – and a cultural sensibility into *Scree*.

Despite the continuities and rhythms in *Scree*, the work in this volume is difficult to neatly compartmentalize or periodize – it is of its time, but as in all of Wah's work, it is not reductive *of* a time. As I am shaping this introduction as a "reader's manual," there is a temptation to map a trajectory of Wah's poetic works that could clearly identify stages that reflect different moments of poetic approach and attention alongside the way his work weaves its way through social and cultural contexts. Such a mapping would trace how the poems uproot certain concepts about nature, language, and identity and lay claim to complex engagements with the meanings of place, the difficulty of identity, and belonging. Yet this approach is thwarted both by Wah's consistent pressuring of poetic form that pushes language to the edge of intelligibility where meaning both brightly disperses and surprisingly coheres, and by the complexity of the historical moment that the poetry is both critical of and in dialogue with. As the works in this volume show us, Wah's poetry from the 1960s through to the 1990s is grounded in particular ways that create a consistent approach or *texture* within the poems even as the poems themselves open to new concerns, places, and literary forms. Given this emphasis on process and change, it is tempting to read Wah's poetry through the opening lines of Charles Olson's "The Kingfishers": "What does not change / is the will to change" (*Collected*, 84). Like the core principle within Olson's memorable line, a truly dynamic aspect of Wah's poetry and poetics has been its engagement with the poetic and the political, the aesthetic and the social, and the ecological and the human, but without building philosophical or linguistic firewalls between them. However, as Louis Cabri points out, this emphasis on the mutability of poetry, place, and history is tied to an expansive relationship to knowledge that represents a reworking of a concept from Olson: "Olson's poetry and poetics greatly appealed to Wah for many reasons, not least because Olson tried to get out of what he called 'the Western box' of assumptions about the world, such as the assumptions governing the Self's relations to (and with) the Other" (xii). This push against the "Western box," along with the influence of an experimental ethnopoetics best exemplified at the time by Jerome Rothenberg's *Shaking the Pumpkin* anthology (1972) and with the ways in which Wah turned to non-Western poetic forms (such as the Japanese *haibun* which he uses for "This Dendrite Map: Father/Mother Haibun" (*Waiting for Saskatchewan*, 73*ff*) and the *utaniki* which shape (Fisher, 95) *Grasp the Sparrows Tail* have come to be part of what Wah later defined, in his critical writing from 1984 to 1999, *Faking It: Poetics and Hybridity,* as an "alienethnic poetry" (55).

But, thinking Wah's early work through this idea of pushing back against the Western box of knowledge provides one of several possible trajectories in this collection. This allows a reader to see how Wah's earliest work blurred or even broke down the boundaries between self and nature (or between subject and object more broadly). This poetic move is beautifully pulled off in the poem "Mountain" which begins, "Mountain that has come over me in my youth" and then accumulates (the image of scree again?) shared histories to the point where the mountain is addressed as if in a dialogue: "Hey Mountain there." Most directly, this is stated in "Among" in what remains, for me, one of the most memorable opening sequences in Wah's work:

> The delight of making inner
>
> an outer world for me
>
> is when I tree myself

And, as I will elaborate later, this relationship of inner and outer, as land as a set of relationships, is tested in *Pictograms from the Interior of B.C.*, where Western knowledge starts to be overridden by Indigenous knowledges and signs. In *Scree* we also see the extension of this testing of Western thought in terms of the content of Wah's work, as such boundaries are opened through a familial investigation and a political inflection as Wah turns to unravel his patrilineal history of his father's movement in search of both belonging and labour. The particulars of Wah's father's life are part of a sincere familial narrative, and they simultaneously illuminate a larger narrative of departure, displacement, and the Asian diaspora as well as the race and class relations of North America. Out of this relationship of the particular "information of a life" and the pressures and possibilities of history, Wah has shaped poetics of resistance and intervention. As Wah has written, in 1995, "The writers I'm interested in have always written from an aesthetic and political position of departure, displacement, decolonization, deterritorialization, and so forth... This 'other' space continually generated methods of resistance and intervention" (*Faking It,* 195).

So, while I do not want to break the work collected in *Scree* into discrete stages that mark particular moments of transition in the books (they defy this structurally as well, for there is a degree of reworking and reiteration of images, lines, and themes throughout the books collected), I do think it is useful to read these poems both in the details of their poetics – in the word-to-word movement of language, image, and thought – *and* to read them alongside their continuities and coalitions.[2] The coalitions that inform this work, and which the poetry draws a certain kind of dialogue from, are the communities and poetics and literary movements that Wah has been associated with and instrumental to. The continuities are the concerns, themes, and poetics that are reworked throughout the books; these give *Scree* multiple narratives of place and movement, clusters of images, and philosophical and linguistic propositions that at times intersect or crystallize through poetic turns and at other times run parallel, adding to the texture of the book even when coherence or closure is strategically avoided. Wah's poetry is remarkably *coherent* even as the poems themselves never tie up neatly.

A continuity that runs through *Scree*, and one that has been a frame for reading Wah's work since *Tish*, is the concept of place. In many ways, the engagement with the landscape of southern British Columbia and the local has remained a signature aspect of Wah's work and along with other poets such as Daphne Marlatt, Roy Kiyooka, George Bowering, Barry McKinnon, Brian Fawcett, Pat Lowther, and Sharon Thesen in British Columbia; Eli Mandel, Robert Kroetsch, Dennis Cooley, and Andy Suknaski in the Prairies; and Christopher Dewdney and David McFadden in Ontario. At the same time, Canadian visual artists were also reworking the representation of landscape through new aesthetic approaches: the N.E. Thing Company's Conceptual approaches, which deconstructed the naturalness of landscape with works such as *Bagged Landscape* (1966); the investigations of the local by London, Ontario-based artist Greg Curnoe; Joyce Wieland's installation work or her bookwork, *True Patriot Love* (1971), which brought a ecological and feminist sensibility to the representation of landscape; and the hard-edged abstraction of painter and printmaker Takao Tanabe (whose print, *Envelope Sketch*, from 1967, is on the cover of *Scree*). Coming from the influences of New American poetry, Wah, formulated a poetics of place and an investigation of localized history drawn from the poetry of William Carlos Williams, Charles Olson, and Ed Dorn. But rather than simply transplanting American poetics onto Canadian soil, as the charge against the *Tish* poets went at the height of Canadian cultural nationalism, Wah reworks the investigative and process-based aspects of these early 1960s poetics through the geographical and cultural details of a different place, a body with a different history that in itself troubled the geographical space of the nation, and through an inquisitive and vibrant poetics syntax, a syntax driven by the "music at the heart of thinking."[3] Just as the concept of place and space was being reworked in other cultural fields, there is a development from a position exclaimed in *Earth,* "I think earth is a condition of ourselves we all have access to," to more a more specific ecopoetics. Looked at within this cultural context, and reread through the poems in *Scree*, place and landscape for Wah are perhaps better understood as both a metabolist and materialist vision. This understanding of the "production of nature," as the geographer Neil Smith puts it, is metabolist in the sense that nature is never passive in Wah's poetry as it is both acted on by society and it also acts on society and the individual, psychically and in terms of perception. For instance, in the short yet beautifully constructed poem "Forest" from *Among*, a syntactic shift stages the people in the poem as agents looking at the forest, yet the forest is also "looking / surrounding":

> And we just stood there
> in the Forest
> look
> at everything around us
> looking
> surrounding

Here nature is not the object of an all-knowing human eye, of a scopic regime – it is not a vista simply looked at – nor is it the foreboding presence that taps into colonial fears of an unknown and hostile landscape. Rather than a split between external nature and human nature, Wah situates a "self amidst the flux of nature," as Brian Kim Stefans has pointed out (92).

Similarly, Cynthia Sugars argues that, in *Diamond Grill*, "Wah plays with the notion of place as a space that both grounds and disrupts identificatory structures" (30). As I think the work in *Scree* shows, this tendency also runs through Wah's earlier work as the ways in which identity take shape and play out in relationship to place and nature. While the critical focus on Wah's later work (from *Diamond Grill* forward) has tended to look at how the complexities of a hyphenated identity are lived, felt, and perceived, this critical reception has generally excluded issues of class and labour. But, in *Scree*, the materialist aspects of nature are best shown when labour is what shapes the relationship between human beings and nature (Smith, 51) – identity, place, and labour are then linked as a relationship. In "Don't Cut Me Down" from *Tree*, a working-class voice chews out what we imagine to be the poet who is more concerned with an idealist nature, hoping to write about the trees from an aesthetic distance: "I don't want any of this tree poetry shit from you." Instead, the poet is told that "Settin chokers'd break your ass so fast you wouldn't want to look at a goddamned tree let alone write about em. Then you'd know what a tree wuz, stead yappin about it." Far from being a parody of a working-class voice, or of working-class knowledge, this poem exactly sets up the tension between an idealized "first nature" and a "second nature" that has been produced through human activity and the exchange of natural resources to surplus capital. In this case, a tree is a complex thing, just as place is.

Moving beyond an idealized nature, Peter Jaeger makes a compelling argument for Wah's work to be seen as a shift from 1960s nature-based poetry, exemplified by Gary Snyder's poetry, which tries to stage a return to a first nature, to an ecopoetical approach, which Jonathan Skinner emphasizes as process-based (128), a poetics that both represent and use "entropy, transformation and decay" (Jaeger, 203). Offering a reading that traces ecopoetics and ethnopoetics as continuities in Wah's work, Jaeger argues, "place in Wah is constructed as the site of both racial and ecological struggle, and his texts offer readers a location for reflecting on the ethical links between ethnopoetics and ecopoetics" (207). Adding to the idea of place as the intersection of the ecological and identity, one way to see the continuities in Wah's notion of place is to look at place as a set of cultural, social, economic, and aesthetic relations rather than a landscape split between first and second nature or between figure and ground. Place becomes a set of relations that in turn produces relationships.

Out of this, place in Wah's work also emerges as a form of knowledge. This approach is most clearly worked out in *Pictograms from the Interior of B.C.*, a book in which Wah sets short texts in relation to Indigenous pictographs, or rock paintings, that were catalogued and documented by John Corner in his book *Pictographs (Indian Rock Paintings) in the Interior of British Columbia* (1968). Wah's *transcreations* (a term that he adapts from Samuel Taylor Coleridge) can be seen as part of his poetics that push against Western knowledge as the hegemonic knowledge for grasping and framing place and history. Read today, fortunately in a time when the cultural appropriation (and cultural dispossession) of Indigenous art and knowledge meets intense resistance, the poems in *Pictograms from the Interior of B.C.* appear as an engagement with a place-based knowledge that is not rooted in the Western separation of first and second nature, nor reliant on the transformation of nature from use value to surplus value or profit (the metaphysics of capitalism). Wah's poems do not try to force the rock paintings into a Western frame by "reading" them as translatable texts (which would assume the smooth transfer of meaning from one knowledge form to another). Rather Wah uses this process of transcreation to test a relational sense of place that troubles the subject/object separation of Western philosophy *in relation* to Indigenous knowledges of land and place that the pictographs represent. Dene scholar Glen Coulthard argues that "it is a profound misunderstanding to think of land or place as simply some material object of profound importance to Indigenous cultures (although it is that too); instead it ought to be understood as a field of 'relationships of things to each other'" (61). These relations also hold ethical obligations, Coulthard emphasizes, "to the land, to animals, plants, and lakes in much the same way that we hold obligations to other people" (ibid.). Wah does not try to impose a "profound misunderstanding" onto the pictographs in the guise of legibility: rather he approaches them as alternative forms of knowledge that cannot be directly translated but which can be understood to hold both an alternative knowledge of place and an "alternative materialist philosophy."[4] Place and land as contested sites of knowledge, of labour, and of identity therefore tie into an expansive poetics that tests received knowledge. In "Reading Asian American Poetry," Juliana Chang asserts, "One way that poetic discourse performs critique is through the construction of alternative forms and structures that simultaneously reveal and disrupt more socially dominant structures" (94). This testing of knowledge is a poetic impulse in postwar North American poetry (a period populated with avant-gardes, critical challenges to national canons, the consolidation of minor literatures, and countercultural formations) as part of a particular tendency, as Chang argues, within North American Asian poetry.

Lastly, I want to locate the poetry of Fred Wah in relation to the communities, cultural formations, and poetics groupings that have influenced his work across the three decades covered in *Scree.* From the early 1960s to the early 1990s, Wah's engagements traverse three North American avant-garde movements and the consolidation of Asian writing in North America as a critical and aesthetic force. By "avant-garde" I mean here a community of writers joined through a shared aesthetic approach as well as an oppositional position in relation to the dominant or prevailing poetry within their national literature. A narrative of Wah's affiliations and dialogues troubles several splits that run through conceptualizations of North American avant-garde formations and the reception of minority writers. Wah's work also disrupts a narrative in which, "The reduction of the cultural politics of racialized ethnic groups, like Asian Americans, to first generation/second generation struggles displaces social differences into a privatized familial opposition" (63), as Lisa Lowe puts it. Familial relations are never displaced from a material history within Wah's work; rather the complexity of poetic form engages with a history of spatial and cultural displacement.

From the *Tish* poets' reworking of the poetics of New American poetry (which lead them to be accused of being a "branch plant" of New American poetics) (Tallman, 115), through the Canadian avant-garde of the 1970s and 1980s that pressured national imperatives through post-structural, feminist, and postmodern perspectives, to the politically inflected project of the language poets, which was itself opened up to a stronger transnational perspective by the New Poetics Colloquium (1985) in Vancouver, to the post-language terrain of the late 1980s, where the potential of the open text was tested across communities, Wah's affiliations are varied yet follow a trajectory of possibility and critique. Alongside this narrative of Wah's work there is both the evolution of nature poetry to ecopoetics and the assemblage of Asian Canadian literature (also in relation to Asian American literature) that develops internally, and in relation to state discourse and literary canon formation, within Canada from the late 1960s. These coalitions – which I see as a joining of poetic communities with the urgency of a social question of a political moment – are assertions of a social and aesthetic grouping. As Timothy Yu has pointed out, "The coalitions imagined by post-1970 American avant-gardes, from Language writers to Asian American poets, are based not on broad appeals to national values but on the means by which each avant-garde delineates its own status as social fact" (39). More forcefully, the coalitions between these avant-gardes were their "critiques" (87) (as Juliana Chang states) of national values that are universalized and therefore exclude communities that fall outside of the constructed unity. Avant-gardes such as the language poets shared aesthetic tactics and linguistic politics with Asian writers who fought against what Roy Miki has described as the imperative to conform to "transparent literary expectations" ("Asiancy," n.p. [8 pages in]). Language itself was staged as a site of struggle rather than as a means of recognition and assimilation.[5]

Yet, despite these coalitions in Wah's writing life, as Donald C. Goellnicht observed recently, "The majority of the criticism on Wah's poetry still places it in a tradition that grows out of the *Tish* movement and includes poets such as George Bowering, bpNichol, Daphne Marlatt, Nicole Brossard, Steve McCaffery, and the language poets" (84). It is because Wah's influences and dialogues cross *Tish*, the language poets, and Asian Canadian writing that his poetry challenges the limitations of the reading and reception of minority writers as well as the avoidance of the social impulse within some avant-garde formations. That the criticism on Wah's work isolates this "experimental" tendency in the poetry, or at least enacts a split between the early experimental poems and the later work that approaches the complexities of identity through a more direct syntax, is reflective of a divide that limits an understanding of the full complexities of minority writers. In her critique of "the unspeakability of race" (23) from critics of the avant-garde, Dorothy Wang has written that:

> Critics of avant-garde writing, despite their openness to radical new poetic forms, often fall into the same traps as more formally conservative critics when thinking (or more accurately, not thinking) the link between poetry and subjectivity which includes the racialized subjectivity – of the poet. They overwhelmingly tend to ignore race by focusing exclusively on formal properties or other themes in writing...; to explicitly oppose political and social "content" (including racial identity) against formal literary concerns; or to distinguish between "bad" ethnic writing (autobiographical, identity-based) and "good" poetry (formally experimental) that just happens to be written by a person of color. (31)

This separation of subjectivity and form only functions if there is an aesthetic distancing to poetic form – that somehow the formal decisions a poet makes are not shaped by social context of the particularities of subjectivity – which codes formally innovative writing as racially unmarked. Curiously, this tends to re-enact a form and content split – the very gap that Wah's work has always troubled. However, as I think is *readable* across *Scree*, formal innovation and poetic decisions are *tactics* that are never at an aesthetic distance from the texture of the immediate social environment, the discourses of governmentality, and the close concerns of the local and community – whether those discourses are politics of recognition driven by official multiculturalism which took shape over the 1970s and 1980s or the immigration and labour policies that shaped the diasporic life of Fred Wah's father.

In a recent interview, in which he replied to a question about his recent role as the Canadian Parliamentary Poet Laureate (from 2011–2013), Fred Wah remarked, "I chose poetry as a reactive practice (anticolonial, grounded in the local, reclamation, etc.). Being close to 'governance' in my Parliamentary Poet Laureate role only confirmed for me the need to insist on a poetry that sustains the imagination of a better world" (mclennan, *Jacket 2,* March 5, 2015). The poems in *Scree* show how the groundwork for this relationship of poetry and the imagination was built up through Wah's engagement with the local as well as poetic influences that crossed borders. The real weight of the poems, or their "purchase" as Robert Creeley might call it, is in their attention to all of the sensual, syntactical, and semantic aspects of language so that the relationship of "governance" and "the imagination of another world" are brought together through the details of a life. Poetry becomes a mapping, an act of the imagination, and a restless, critical form of knowledge.

I'd like to thank Fred Wah and Pauline Butling for the discussions we had in shaping *Scree* and in situating Fred's work in its cultural context. Louis Cabri supplied key editorial suggestions to this text and, as always, sharpened the critical take. Thanks as well to Amy Johal and Stephen Collis for feedback on the introduction, to Ryan Fitzpatrick and friends at the Wah site for the bibliography and for PDF facsimiles, and to Ann-Marie Metten and Greg Gibson at Talonbooks for their always excellent editing work.

—JEFF DERKSEN

Vancouver, April 2015 – Aigen, Austria, August 2015

Endnotes

1 This statement can also be considered in relation to Robert Kroetsch's essay "Disunity as Unity: a Canadian Strategy" (1989).

2 I am adapting the framework that Larissa Lai has recently proposed for a reading of Canadian Asian literature as a coalitional practice rather than a genealogy. "While there has been a tendency, certainly at present, but also at various historical moments to posit a linear and heroic history for Asian Canadian literature, I argue that it is in rupture and coalition that the term has been most generative" (1). Likewise, Guy Beauregard suggests a similar idea in his introduction to the Asian Canadian Studies issue of *Canadian Literature* (199, Winter 2008): "There's no single running track here and, given the complexity of contemporary social formations and historical and cultural representations, no set end point to contemporary Asian Canadian critical projects, whose points of engagement continue to be multiple and varied" (11).

3 *Music at the Heart of Thinking* is the title of a long-running series of poems as syntactical blasts of critical language that Wah has been working on since the mid-1980s.

4 In an essay that lays a ground for an intersectional engagement with Indigenous knowledges, Larissa Lai proposes two questions: "First, what could a politics and practice of respect look like for Asian Canadians engaged and implicated in a settler culture? And second, for Asian Canadians who occupy the contradictory site of both settler and colonial subject, what can we contribute towards turning the world to respectful balance?" ("Epistemologies of Respect," 102). What I'm emphasizing is that Wah's engagement with Indigenous knowledge is also based on an anti-colonial poetics that is at the basis of both his poetics that work against the Eurocentric confinement of knowledge (the Western box) and an aspect of some Asian North American writing. This engagement has not always been at the level of content; it has been a part of Wah's formal approach to poetics. That is, it is form that can also make a poetics anti-colonial or oppositional.

For a discussion in a parallel field, see Horton and Berlo, "Beyond the Mirror," 28.

5 At this moment it is difficult to frame any present avant-gardist tendency as positive or oppositional. The turn against avant-gardist formation in activist politics, the institutionalization of previous avant-gardes, and the recent crystallizing of a white supremacist avant-gardism have all ignited a new scrutiny of avant-gardist tendencies. See Ken Chen's "Authenticity Obsession, or Conceptualism as Minstrel Show" on the Asian American Writers' Workshop website and "Avant-Garde Forum" in *Lana Turner* 7.

Works Cited

Beauregard, Guy. "Asian Canadian Studies: Unfinished Projects." *Canadian Literature* 199 (Winter 2008): 6–27.

Bowering, George. "The Poems of Fred Wah." Introduction, *Loki Is Buried at Smoky Creek*. Vancouver: Talonbooks, 1980.

Cabri, Louis. *The False Laws of Narrative: The Poetry of Fred Wah*. Waterloo, ON: Wilfrid Laurier University Press, 2009.

Chang, Juliana. "Reading Asian American Poetry." *Melus* 21.1 (Spring 1996): 81–98.

Corner, John. *Pictographs (Indian Rock Paintings) in the Interior of British Columbia*. Vernon: Wayside Press, 1968.

Coulthard, Glen. *Red Skin, White Masks: Rejecting the Colonial Politics of Recognition*. Minneapolis: University of Minnesota Press, 2014.

Derksen, Jeff. "Making Race Opaque: Fred Wah's Poetics of Opposition and Differentiation." *West Coast Line* 29.3 (1995–96): 63–76.

Dobson, Kit. *Transnational Canadas: Anglo-Canadian Literature and Globalization*. Waterloo, ON: Wilfrid Laurier Press, 2009.

Fisher, Susan. "Japanese Elements in the Poetry of Fred Wah and Roy Kiyooka." *Canadian Literature* 163 (Winter 1999): 93–110.

Goellnicht, Donald C. "Asian Kanadian, Eh?" *Canadian Literature* 199 (Winter 2008): 71–99.

Horton, Jessica L., and Janet Catherine Berlo, "Beyond the Mirror: Indigenous Ecologies and 'New Materialisms' in Contemporary Art." *Third Text* 27:1 (2013): 17–28.

Jaeger, Peter. "Ethnicity, Ecopoetics, and Fred Wah's Biotext," *Journal of Postcolonial Writing* 46.2 (2010): 199–208.

Kroetsch, Robert. "Disunity as Unity: a Canadian Strategy." *The Lovely Treachery of Words*. Toronto: Oxford University Press, 1989.

Lai, Larissa. *Slanting I, Imagining We: Asian Canadian Literary Production in the 1980s and 1990s*. Waterloo, ON: Wilfrid Laurier Press, 2014.

____. "Epistemologies of Respect: A Poetics of Asian / Indigenous Relations." In *Critical Collaborations: Indigeneity, Diaspora, and Ecology in Canadian Literary Studies*, edited by Smaro Kamboureli and Christl Verduyn, 99–126. Waterloo, ON: Wilfrid Laurier University Press, 2014.

Lefebvre, Henri. *Rhythmanalysis: Space, Time, and Everyday Life*. New York: Continuum, 2004.

Lowe, Lisa. *Immigrant Acts: On Asian American Cultural Politics*. Durham: Duke University Press, 1996.

mclennan, rob. "Short Interview with Fred Wah." *Jacket 2: Some Notes on Canadian Poetry* (blog), March 5, 2015.

Miki, Roy. "Global Drift: Thinking the Beyond Identity Politics." *Canadian Literature* 199 (Winter 2008): 144–157.

____. "Asiancy: Making Space for Asian Canadian Writing." *Broken Entries: Race, Subjectivity, Writing*. Toronto: Mercury Press, 1998.

Olson, Charles. *Collected Poems of Charles Olson: Excluding* The Maximus Poems. Edited by George F. Butterick. Berkeley: University of California Press, 1987.

Palmer, Bryan D. *Canada's Sixties: The Ironies of Identity in a Rebellious Era.* Toronto: University of Toronto Press, 2009.

Rothenberg, Jerome. *Shaking the Pumpkin: Traditional Poetry of the Indian North Americas.* Barrytown, NY: Station Hill, 2014 (1972).

Rudy, Susan, "Fred Wah – Among," *Writing in Our Time: Canada's Radical Poetries in English (1957–2003).* Waterloo, ON: Wilfrid Laurier University Press, 2005.

Skinner, Jonathan. "Statement for 'New Nature Writing'." *Ecopoetics* 4.5 (2004–5): 127–29.

Smith, Neil. *Uneven Development: Nature, Capital, and the Production of Space.* Athens, GA: University of Georgia Press, 2008 (1984).

Stefans, Brian Kim. "Remote Parsee: An Alternative Grammar of Asian North American Poetry." *Telling It Slant: Avant-Garde Poetics of the 1990s.* Edited by Mark Wallace and Steven Marks. Tuscaloosa: University of Alabama Press, 2001. 43–75.

Sugars, Cynthia. " 'The Negative Capability of Camouflage': Fleeing Diaspora in Fred Wah's *Diamond Grill.*" *Studies in Canadian Literature* 26.1 (2001): 27–45.

Tallman, Warren. "A Brief Retro-Introduction to *Tish.*" *Beyond Tish: New Writing, Interviews, Critical Essays.* Edited by Douglas Barbour. Spec. issue of *West Coast Line* 25.1 (1991): 115–119.

Yu, Timothy. *Race and the Avant-Garde: Experimental and Asian American Poetry Since 1965.* Stanford, CA: Stanford University Press, 2009.

Wah, Fred. *Lardeau.* Toronto: Island, 1965.

___. *Mountain.* Buffalo, NY: Audit/East-West, 1967.

___. *Among.* Toronto: Coach House, 1972.

___. *Tree.* Vancouver: Vancouver Community, 1972.

___. *Earth.* Canton, NY: Institute of Further Studies, 1974.

___. *Pictograms from the Interior of B.C.* Vancouver: Talonbooks, 1975.

___. *Loki Is Buried at Smoky Creek: Selected Poems.* Vancouver: Talonbooks, 1980.

___. *Breathin' My Name with a Sigh.* Vancouver: Talonbooks, 1981.

___. *Owners Manual.* Lantzville, BC: Island Writing Series, 1981.

___. *Grasp the Sparrow's Tail.* Kyoto: Nagata Bunshodo, 1982.

___. *Waiting for Saskatchewan.* Winnipeg: Turnstone, 1985.

___. *Music at the Heart of Thinking.* Red Deer, AB: Red Deer College Press, 1987.

___. *Rooftops.* Nobleboro, ME: Blackberry Books, 1987, and Red Deer, AB: Red Deer College Press, 1988.

___. *So Far.* Vancouver: Talonbooks, 1991.

___. *Faking It: Poetics and Hybridity, Critical Writing 1984–1999.* Edmonton: NeWest Press, 2000.

Wang, Dorothy. *Asian American: Thinking Its Presence: Form, Race, and Subjectivity in Contemporary Asian American Poetry.* Stanford, CA: Stanford University Press, 2014.

Yu, Timothy. *Race and the Avant-Garde: Experimental and Asian American Poetry Since 1965.* Stanford, CA: Stanford University Press, 2009.

A Note

In collating this work I have left the poems pretty much as they were published originally, except to correct spelling and minor variances of punctuation or formatting, and to tweak a few words or lines. Doing this revealed to me the iteration, repetition, and shaping that were part of the shifting modes and opportunities of production since the early 1960s. In this broader recuperation of the poetry, I saw that my writing had been generated in the context of hands-on, small-press publishing; in other words, an exploration of the book as a frame for a particular community; a public invested in opening an aesthetic of otherness. This collection extends that kind of activity to pose yet another repositioning, within the context of the Talonbooks collected poems series.

As I sifted through the writing of these early years, each book re-presented its own making. *Lardeau* was typed out on mimeograph stencils in Toronto with Victor Coleman's IBM Selectric and printed by him as *Island* 4. Then, in Buffalo, fellow grad students Al Glover and George Butterick did a hand-bound lithographed edition of *Mountain.* Coach House Press, so central to the production of a major portion of Canadian poetry, gave *Among* a glassine cover and printed the poems with a leafy background (part of the innovative but short-lived Wallpaper series). *Tree* was part of Vancouver Community Press's Writing Series. I typed the plates using the large-font typewriter from Meadow Creek Elementary School while Lauren (Bird) Hamilton made the drawings, and then it was printed on the offset press in Argenta, British Columbia. The fascicle *Earth* was actually an assignment for *A Curriculum of the Soul*, mimeographed for the Institute of Further Studies in Canton, New York, by Al Glover, with cover by Guy Berard. Provincial apiarist John Corner was gracious in sharing with me his work on indigenous pictographs for my transcreative project *Pictograms from the Interior of B.C.*, the first of many of my books sustained by Karl Siegler and Talonbooks. John Marshall and Daphne Marlatt published my extension of the pictograms, *Owners Manual*, for their Island Writing Series using the lovely letterpress work of Morriss Printing in Victoria. bpNichol's editing and compositional smarts were crucial in helping me manoeuvre the biotextual turn of *Breathin' My Name with a Sigh*. When we lived in Kyoto in 1982 I negotiated with Nagata Bunshodo a self-published edition of *Grasp the Sparrow's Tail* bound in traditional four-eye binding. And by the time Dennis Cooley asked for *Waiting for Saskatchewan* for Turnstone Press in 1984, the small presses of the 1970s had become the perfect-bound mainstays of a groundswell of poetry publishing. The point is, for me, making poetry has always remained local and part of a conversation with a community whose belief in taking the work into their own hands is fundamental not just to making art but to making a world worth living in.

Besides this community of publishers and editors, I'd like to thank Jeff Derksen for helping to shape this *Scree*, and I'd like to particularly thank Greg Gibson for his close editing and guidance and Les Smith for layout and design. Thanks to everyone at Talonbooks for their continuing support and representation of my work.

—FRED WAH
August 2015

(FROM)

TISH

(1962–1963)

THE MING TREE

Never having climbed
a Ming tree, Hong
refused membership
in our tree house.

Nor would he slide
on the icy hill
beneath it
during the winter.

That was thirteen years ago.
I was home last month
and the snow was
a foot deep on its roof.

A TESTIMONY

I

out here on sloping seaward mountains
tides
and salt, fish smell comes
from the west to the west

washed wood on beaches
(cut clay drifts
to abide the sand)

sunken chain/rusted/galvanized
sewer pipes

oil twigs glass grass
of the sea out west
for the west
/always has
come
Juan de Fuca junk stream
for the meeting twain

ALL tied into the trade
(winds Indian monsoons)

even Chinese junks washed up/sent back
years ago

I can see it from these beaches
ends of mountain forests force back
into the sea

it's as far as they came, the traders
over the mountain streams, the Fraser
flowing into the sea and held
here held

where the west is the west and the east
suppressed
into churning Strait of Georgia
washed up

for the seagulls
(white gluttons of the treasure)

from the mountains/for the sea

II

I have seen it
to see with

(There are more suicides per capita in the west coast cities than anywhere else in North America. Psychiatrists tell us that this is partly due to the psychological impact of the phrase "go west, young man." The young man goes west for success and when he doesn't achieve it commits suicide from one of the many success-symbol bridges)
death in my eyes.

I came out
to big coast town
where the rain washes
away

under concrete bridges
under cloudy skies
and the moist bark
of dogwood
I cried
and the tears
/washed into the sea
down sandy 10th Avenue gutters

trickling, and it went on
like the jazz and basement dwellings
broken water heaters
dreams
and boulevards in the fog

but the sea
returned the sea
into broken waves

and reverberates
in quiet pools
on the wet sand
still
out
on West Point Grey/in love of it

the death of the land
going down to the sea
to the sea
beginning again

III

bury me, not
in the lonely sea

sings to me

though I am born
of east and west
wheat and the wind
in the heat
of flat yellow fields
gophered burrows
in the dried-up
clay of the mind

sings to me
death be not wet

OF A CITY

a black smokestack
sticks straight up
silently
the white smoke
escapes into the grey sky

does actually
become the cloud
for me
or
acts with the wind
on the wind
floats over some drab buildings
disperses...
which is peaceful
to watch

the unheard billowing
broken down
into the dull day
un
exciting
way of the mind
acts on the mind
useless...
silence
broken
by the silence

I shiver
and yawn at the fuming structure
with
with

•

no end to it
that continual
smoke
drifting

drives the man
into himself
and always then
to the water

THE SCAFFOLDING

The scaffolding
is a caging in
of the nearly finished building

it is a pipe-and-board jungle
gawping cubes of space
streaked with wet cement droppings

and the workmen strut and shout
erect assurance
of the solidity
of early-morning air

FOCAL: TO KINGFISHER

November 7, 1962, 8:20 p.m.

in the dark glass
here are words
that are light
the distance: time

the lapse: interval
cracked
                beyond the window
                headlights stream
                flipped into eyes

: dream

the left hand with the gold band
on the fourth finger to the outside

I do not write you with no occasion
the dream is in the water, remember
which is sometimes felt with eyes
what has happened is dreamt often

& one sees in dreams & I saw you
twisting that ring with your right fingers
and remembering thought of Beth
who was, in a way, seemed part of

the story:
               went away
                      with the sound
           in my mind
                               smoothing
                     something like seas
                                         making the bent
                  that way
                                pointing ship
                      out for a week
                           at a single time
         amongst other men
                                         & thoughtless
                     I heard
                            of safety

soon felt the feet
& this is what the others could watch for themselves

(revised from a thought several weeks back)

thinking of
the little song:

"kingfishers catch fire"
fisherMan sockeye
towboats drop chains ...
boxcars
hobo knows
what He's doin'

see, the thought sees

Samson in the window
made out of distance
standing your words
on vibrating air & on air
between the darker trees
my eyes with some words still in them
after you went

here is some sort of singing – humming in the dark glass

THE TRANSFERENCE

take the sea
& gulls rising
  the distance &
stand in the forest

with love and her breath
inside as growing roots move
you as reaching
into your own mind's dream
                    stretch
                              out in the grass
                    come
sit in this room of remembrances
back over mountains . green
in the valleys
a tree of coloured leaves
& paths
               were it only all
               this the poem is
               after all, and it is

these transferents
that make my mind up
of each day's goodness

                 ripeness is
a falling

the ground gets hard by frost
& all these
                 to have the seasons
                 to have what comes
                 to have my love

snatched from the moon
with the hand

THE RABBIT

is dead
I wonder, still there
in moss over large
fields patch fur
red clots, muddy
bed in peat

do you know
of peat moss
how it grows
under rain like
rice paddies
caked then, in the sun
so soft and dry
enough for sleeping
on under summer stars,
stumps a thousand years
old growing as the fields
sink around them

then one late August
afternoon with my shift
shift tractor cleats
spitting up sphagnum
in the corner, field
edged with ditch
I spun & missed
dead rabbit
trick of twist
twist tracks
in the dust

MY HORSE

I never had
who carries me
so secretly
is dead

I think
he bucked
& threw me
on a mountain
at the bottom
of the path

O my dead horse
I never had
such dreams
as dreams of you
not there
when I ride past

FORDORN

as it is
sitting with your voice
at my ear
hearing you the day after
you've gone

    (we lack stillness
    past the sack curtain
    the street of concrete
    moving cars
    repeats the picture

    a lack of stillness)

still
there you are
with a soft voice
softly you cowboy
are here
or wherever
now

you came and went
became a remnant
or remembering
mere memory
but you've gone

& I went with you
which learning one could
always wait for, waiting for
a soft voice at my ear
back & forth across the country

which geographies & indians therein
became my own north idaho montana
& all boundaries of which
I too do bounce against
mindfully and otherwise

(though you, or I rather
could not take the sage smoke
which so filled this particular summer
you now lead me back to
& were you in Kalispell that July
from which town the yanks got wind of
the fire which crowned miles across tamarack
with a strong southerly
and caught me pissing at the border fence
into Montana on such a hot Saturday afternoon?

& I certainly do wish
we should stop for a beer
at either Elko/Whitefish tavern
& reminisce about
just this particular fire)

but you've gone
really
& a lack of stillness
pervades the lighted night streets
and this my dream or thought
which you brought
in a so-soft voice

as it is
it is with
this hearing you
the day after

(FROM)

Lardeau

(1965)

THE SEANCERS AT DEANSHAVEN

On a hill above green water
which is a lake runs by
becoming a river down or
further off to the south

still within this green valley
because it is July
left on the hill to the right
of Deanshaven among trees

he
is a painter
of reason
for cash of his rococo things

and there for magical purposes
it is he and his friends' hill

and I and my wife
are on ours
as there is that renewal each summer
to look down upon the lake

what ritual on the other side
for evening thunderclouds
to ride us both as rails
down the range of peaks
which cup the lake going south

the lightning
cuts up the dark valleys
reveals them dancing among tall trees
their cabins the mysterious
rococo canvasses jump
to the forks of the sky fire too

and it ends with the night
where we in the Queens Bay orchard stand
I come into myself with the mountains
dark paintings fall into me
across the green water on this side.

ARBUTUS ISLAND, AS I SEE IT

the first time
that tree softened
(in the mind)

the regular tundra
of my common hillsides

escorted by a man, Goody
through, on a Sunday
the bottom half island

struck
by an arbutus tree
in the town, Ganges
gave way on a corner
suddenly
                though

for the better stuff inland
which, to be taken in quietly
was soft

in the distance of their groves
peeling
to go on
                seeing

red paper reaped
by the smoothest cut
I'd let on to be
thinking about.

THE FIGURING

in your mother's garden
last summer
the peas
& the feel of a pod in my hand
there were bells clanging
& the uncovering
separating
shells

we came down
the west side
on the continent
believing it was ocean
it was land
leaving our forests
(our forests
& turned left
on a desert
at moonlight
alone
the sound
in my throat
half-stuck
ringing song-like
in the trees
(the proof is
was what
once was

& you naked
in the back seat
sleeping
the flat headlights
on either side
the cacti
became darknesses
rising
in the heat
the hot flatness
is us naked
here

(once
the trees hid us
from the moon & the lake
& I filled you

sweet granite boulders
which will suck this step
back quick
to the rock's warmth
& melt at the snow's
edge
which
is called
into the crevasse
by thinking back

the flat
between my seeing
I was riding
up
the middle
out
between the distant mountains
a rock
a wedge
coming back for myself
with you
flat out
behind my eyes

miles
is what was
the road sign says
(said) when looking back-
wards back up the road
where we'd come from
with nothing from the land with us
& we're all there is here
& saying that is too hard
is like trying to

think mountain-like
add up, figure
out
the haziness
our forests
our nakedness
& a way of looking at signposts
but all myself
turning back into
standing
up
along the pea vines
& peeling them
they rolled into the bowl
following one, one, one,
clanging bell-like
in my throat
on the desert.

THE OCTOBER ARGUMENT

She says that I cling to the past
trees, places, people, and things
but my cheeks are cold
in the walk around the block
tonight

we are both here together
now what more is present
than a memory
my cheeks get warmer
and the darkness is out there

my love there is no compromise
if you will not wait
while I drag my ass
in the past.

MOON DOG

the dog barks
on another street

two dogs bark
& the one in the sky

the stars
all bark at

the moon

stop yapping
& it hides in the mountains

EYES

Dog with three legs
with a name as round as
his head is as round
as his eyes are

his many
many other
                    bignesses
                                        his eyes
          come into
                              his eyes, look
                                            at you, you
                                            look back
howling
at the moon
in the morning
                        the moon
                        his big sky-eye

                        & wooing
                        at the sun
dog
with three legs
behind you
when you run he looks

for the stick you've thrown
hit

all falls into his eyes

                  his paws
                  his other
                            or
                  eyes are

                  his many
                  many other

ACROBAT ON A BALL

the boy stands
balanced on a ball
which does not move

the man
sits on a blue cloth
on a blue box
which does not move

on a hill behind
the woman
& two children
with a dog
do not move

a horse eats
on a further hill
but the eating
does not move

& the blue sky
is a blue sky too

behind the last hill
is not there
though a man runs
down a mountain path
which ends
when he steps into
a dark forest

the tall trees hide
where he runs on to
& sway in the wind

when the moon begins
by then
the man is not there

though the moon moves
behind the last hill
& the stillness is too

IN THE AFTERNOON, SUNDAY

Glance at its white
not
at its birch bark

where are
the bare grey branches branching
against the spring snow
which is melting

to where they
glance white
in grey bare
air, are dancing
on the hillside

a hill you look up
at the birches in March
which fill
the west side of the mountain
white

or part of a mountain
is part white
and the sun
not part white
at all.

To see this
a mud road
to pull over to
step out on the dirty snow, move
back from you
stop
smile
click
with the sun behind me
as close as I can plot
behind the clouds.

The picture comes out
most white, with a face
somewhere, I
remember the grey
but the trees
are not there.

A FABLE

There somewhere
a big pounded meatball went loping.
As it went loping along the road
one was lying there somewhere beside the road.
The loping one said
to him, that coyote
                                        Are you lying here?
That coyote said
                                        Yes, I am lying here
                                        I am about to die of hunger.
That big meatball
said to him
                          You must take one big bite of me.

And he did take a bite of it
and ran along the road again
stopped and lay down over there
in front of it, the meatball,
where it was rolling here
loping along the road.

And are you lying here?
He is and with hunger also
and so that big meatball said to him
that coyote
                          You must take one big bite of me.

And so he did three times
running down along the road again
to stop and lie down over there wherever
in front of where the rolling was
all the time for one big bite.

Oh, you are that same one
moving along cheating me
for he saw himself
in amongst the coyote's teeth.

THE FIRE

The international border
is a twenty-five-yard cut
out of the green forest

& in the middle
            right in the middle of the cut
is a fence
            made of posts and wire

birds fly
a field hawk
& the pink sky turns brown
                                        sun
                    (crackle crackle
                                        a
wood-burning July afternoon.

          None said of where
          the fire began on the Idaho side
          but by two o'clock three of us laughed
          & pissed across the fence
          to protect?
                        the untouched B.C. tamaracks?

          so soon
          it crowned the twenty-five yards

& I'm running
        to catch a ride out
with the pump truck but
        the hose is caught, round a stump

& he says
        when I'm looking at him
look
        take the axe to it anyway
already the paint's peeling on my side

Beautiful

run because I have to
                                        birds fly & pink smoke
how low the sky comes
                                        the smoke comes

just as fast but low through grass & trunks &
                        run
                         &
                        run
                               &

a man is caught in a hollow
his name is Marvin.

LARDEAU / SUMMER 1964

I said we slept in a shack
at the bottom of the valley
watched the sun set after supper
over an ice field to the north
an unnamed glacier, then
the mountains about us
left white by the moon.

And I said it was a hot day
where we were I had a headache
at noon the blue above turned
to a green blur of moving trees
the felled log rolled under me
and we began the afternoon's cruise
looking at ourselves in the forest.

About the Lardeau?
There is little to say.
It is green, it rains
often, the mountains
are very beautiful,
there is a moon at night,
the unnamed glacier is the shape
of a bird in flight, with stars
in its eyes, my logging boots
make me feel strong
but too heavy to use strength,
the rivers and creeks
flow south to the lake,
there are mosquitoes, the name
is Marblehead.

At the end of it
it was all a dream
I said from looking up
up an eighty-foot pole
at lunch and he:
well, I'll be here all winter
and the cruising's easy on snowshoes
though this summer has been a nice one
gotta get that left shock fixed next time in town

I said
you must be finishing labour
at the top of Meadow Mountain
for she was born at 9:15
and we neared the top then too
I had pains in my stomach.

SHAPE-OF-A-BIRD-WITH-STARS-IN-ITS-EYES

Unnamed glacier
north
25 degrees west
north
look north tonight
at white
the white hump of ice
the moon the snow
bright
shape-of-a-bird-with-stars-in-its-eyes
go morning north
road that way to dawns and breakfasts
morning grass boots wet
and some morning don't stop to eat
with the boots keep walking
ten miles and find out
then go into it and into it
the wet grass morning glacier the
shape-of-a-bird
there where I arrive
with my wet boots on
what should I name it

THE ROADS

All the ways are gravel
        or crushed rock or rock bed
in a pickup truck Al and I
        switchback up the mountain
until we get to the still
        and hot afternoon stopped
on the side of Meadow Mountain
        we mean to locate to a patch
of cedar 3,500 feet away
        at 5 percent and try to stick
to the benches he says though
        I'm slow imagining these trees
make way, as we do, all 'round
        to Gold Hill, Howser, etc.

THE CRUISE

From 6,349 we headed
down S 30° W salmonberry
mountain ash alder then
the damp gullies pulled
out of the 105 chains
by ten, we sweat and puff
alongside a log at the edge
of an old burn, sitting
like that the horseflies
and mosquitoes the green
green leaves, type lines
on the map with a *D*
for "deciduous" 188
chains, down a couple miles
to the jeep by a creek
a drink alone and...

WHEN

When it is hot
when in the afternoon
tomorrow
last night
today when
to expect
the way
to take
(of
the mind's meadows
yes)

I'll drive
to meet you thirty miles
of gravelly dust
greet you with smiles of
I love
and miss you Love
is a kiss
of dusty lips
spill out my heart
to you on this
O yes
I will when it is hot
when in the afternoon
the mind expects.

CLIMB

Climb up get a way through to the top
of this rock face for a view much better
for the possible road into this canyon
no you climb and we'll wait here at the
bottom by the coolness of the creek meet
you in a while sure but the stupidity and
risk to get such a view on the way back down
weak muscles shake feeling a way through
this cliff I freeze on a shelf and cannot
go down and cannot go back up.

AKOKLI (GOAT) CREEK

More music
in its name
than "goat"

Akokli rise
as the June
snow melts.

The forest
is dark above
the road above

the creek
the mountain
moves down

the jeep
moves down
the trees

the dark is
down among

the bumpy swells
of Akokli Creek.

GOLD HILL

We stood there in Gold Hill's forest
        looking
at all that surrounded us
        that rock
this rock here this one
        was it here
he stopped by stooped down aside of
        and grabbed from the rock
a piece of moss to wipe himself with
        said shIT!
this granite boulder's gold
        worth about
as he was an assayer also
        $70,000
but unable to move such a large rock himself
        chipped some proof
then went away to find help
        file the claim
but never found it after that day
        so
we stood there in Gold Hill's forest
        looking.

THEY ARE BURNING

Pitch black up the valley
in front of us twenty miles
they are burning the mountains down
the sky is that kind of orange
the hillsides are outlined to us
in just that orange horizon
which will be gone with daybreak
when the smoke of their burning
hangs over the valleys rivers and trees
drifts slowly on the contours of the land
and the deadness where no birds fly.

Yes they are burning
for it is July
and August and the nights
with no wind the darkness is cool.

What I thought would be there is not
I'm sorry to say. What I had expected
was to sleep for the ride with eyes closed
not drive into a burning mountainside.

MORNING

Up
   the mosquito
prong on the wall
at my head my
head tried in
splendecorous
colours the night's
rainbow slit
in the moon of morning
craving more sleep
and dream
the buzz of wings
sings at my head
my

THE COLD SNOW FEET

The cold snow feet
sweat
with all those clothes on
Eddy Thompson
ahead in the bushes
follow me
or maybe he, Steve Barrett
between the light bush
push
          with one leg
raise a knee
my big snowshoe
dives toe under the snow
toward the creek
which cracks with our weight and the sun
sweat steaming the taste of scarf
we say wobble and run
but I can't but trip
trying to lift one foot
the other sinks
webs dangling in air
I become a ball of white
with all those clothes
and fall on my face
into the dark snow
my sweating face...

Mike
use the shoes
it's night
your skis are iced
from that fall in the lake
Molly Gibson is
how many miles away now
use your shoes Mike
carry the skis
are you alone
how many miles behind us

Drummond Hadley's
snowshoes' tracks
disappear
toward Grover Cleveland Park's
golf course by Main Street
on the desert
coming up (out of) the arroyo
on snowshoes in December
among the galleta grass
like a green winter lawn in Tucson
bowlegged strapped in mukluks
gut web for feet
over all that desert
No

and so there somewhere
the watched bear paws
hang there all summer
there on my head
which is down on the tracks
or sometimes not the tracks
but the sssshhhhhhhh –
in the feet

Mountain

(1967)

Mountain that has come over me in my youth
green grey orange of coloured dreams
darkest hours of no distance
Mountain full of creeks ravines of rock
and pasture meadow snow white ridges humps of granite
ice springs trails twigs stumps sticks leaves moss
shit of bear deer balls rabbit shit
shifts and cracks of glaciation mineral
O Mountain that has hung over me in these years of fiery desire
burns on your sides your many crotches rocked
and treed in silence from the winds
Mountain many voices nameless curves and pocked in shadows
not wild but smooth
your instant flats flat walls of rock
your troughs of shale and bits
soft summer glacier snow
the melting edge of rounded stone
and cutting of your height the clouds
a jagged blue
your nights your nights alone
your winds your winds your grass

your lying slopes your holes your traps
quick blurs of all my dreams
Mountain poem of life
true and real
reeling Mountain burning mind
stand word stand letter
voice in whisper secret repeating cries
stand in rock stretch out
in all ways to the timberline
spread over all valleys run cool the water down
from luminous white snows
your cracks

O creek song flow always an utter pure of coolness
spring from the rocks
sing in the hot thirst my sticky tongue
my jaw catch below the bridge
Yes my jaw for your waters hangs
catch of water soothe the sweat
sweet cold on teeth in flow and eddy
in swirl my gut it fills and bloats with fluid Mountain

White

over

all the air the valley shifts

shift up

the valley's shape over all the cup the earth it makes

of the cottonwood

O the cottonwood

float a hillside up with fluff rise

eyes of the world whirling through me

clamour some sky-like music

fill the currents of the valley white

clumps the eyes of the trees

even slits in her sides dark alder gullies hide under

white fluffs your cotton smooth earth-covered earth

blurry in in

semen spray soft cottonwood cotton

cotton

cotton

cotton

Sludge in the lake bottom right
the Willet
Lardeau
across Argenta
morning
a new town
the mirror of pulled out
to the marsh and the rock bluffs
north

Birds of the Mountain lift me
fill in my eyes the dark-walled places of the sides
the moving airs on rock push up the faces
to the edge I climb
where the birds on the way out
hang
the air which is their own beating
keep the shape of the Mountain
and pull at my arms the edge of ice or rock
and pull out and out on the cool rise
and fill out the spaces to the top rock
the dry ridges the iced ridges
the black crevices green valleys
O shoulders beaks wings legs boots
push out

Wherever you are wherever
you can believe in pictures of the earth's contours
and just because it's dark out have words enough
the earth tonight can't wait –
the moon is gold the stars are
somewhere the snow glitters back the ice shines
a cold moon the white makes
and the eyes of Marblehead take in spaces as deep as their faces
black pit-void voice the mouth hole
the words all are places and distant the snowbird
a bowl to the white moon's brightening

---

fucking brown the fall airs O
the end of August rains turn snow
the dirt is hard around the rocks the leaves are warm
around those rocks the roots are worn the dirt is
O so Co-old

---

even the eyes
along the road the map plots
move as once moved
time took from
even the eyes switch
turn with each bend
bridge the creeks cut
even the eyes the fences make
and lumberyards the sawdust fills
even the eyes scan
along a lake the ditches' bottles weed and beaches' sand
or gravelled air of gravel
even the dust the eyes recall what the map shows
as trail flag stop railway trestle
creosote planks
or power line cut is or clearing the legs' relief
from elevation intervals ridge to ridge
the contour eyes make boundaries shot
chains traverse the timber lease
or lookout eyes look lookout of
even the eyes a lake is or creek fills
and the map the eye is a circle makes
even the Mountain isn't

Hey Mountain there

spring up in the sky my skull holds

a blazing green of scree and trees

Hey your ice your ice

it hides

moves and slides

white and cold as corn of summer smooth the winter's snow becomes

so be your peaks in a very blue sky indeed

squat where the legs of you slope

flower out in the lakes of my eyes shimmering Kootenay waters green

dark green

flow down and into

RISE

BENT

the beat my self my heart's

BENT BENT

Bear system Fur quivering at the tree's roots

not even a growl the gut flowing in cloud

the vaporous red dream the horse's cock

by the field the river

erect to mount the mare

beating

FUR FUR

in the valleys the hot afternoon

the animals screwing

all their mountains all the

Ya Fur Fur

I stand the upright Mountain

at its base I stand in roads in valleys

in standing desire its quieting gravel ways

stand roots upturned at the roadside

turn in and twist deeper the head's nerves

and gentle sinking stump my body

warm

I look out at it to its tree branching

boughs bird's wings

flap in green in sunlight light-brown needles

ground is covered dried shit of deer bed

old

the old tree stand my axe is melting

in bite the grain of the trunk

burning the fire down to its roots black the bark hard

the upright tree the Mountain's burn

look out at it

stand in it turn cover the ground

take off the thought's eyes

go in

go in

go in the flaming base

sink in the skins of the Mountain's earth

along the road

far from the road

in gravel

stand through the twist in desire the gravelled road inward

to the base of the upright Mountain

its quiet burning

it's evening still

it's my eyes have gone my eyes my birds' wings

fluttering

O Mountain stand is set my roots the sun is in my legs

Tree

(1972)

TREE
FRED WAH

TREE

TREE

FRED WAH

Vancouver Community Press

Writing Series No.9

Acknowledgments: Among (Coach House, 1972) Co Tinneh, Free Poems Among Friends, Georgia Straight Writing Supplement, Hamill's Last Stand, Imago, Iron, Magazine of Further Studies, Scree.

Drawings by Bird Hamilton, Argenta, B.C.

Go to the forest, Tree
please wait for me there

DON'T CUT ME DOWN

I don't want any of this tree poetry
shit from you. You don't know what a
fuckin tree is. If ya think its only
in yer head yer full a shit. Trees is
trees and the only thing they're good
for is lumber so don't give me any crap
about them bein sumpin else. Fer chrys
sake you think the rest of us don't
know sweet fuck all compared to you.
Well you don't know nuthin till ya go
out there and bust yer back on em.
Settin chokers'd break yer ass so fast
ya wouldn't even wanna look at a
goddamned tree let alone write about
em. Then ya'd know what a tree wuz,
steda yappin about it.

Tree of colored textured brain
bathed in twisted neural headlights
twined trunk of cedar bark all shaggy
woman man tree
underpits which root me to the image
like a root is
moving through the darkness of the soil
nerves and soul (like baling wire
a line of thought
taut shoots in screaming hot blood leaps
of pool   pool   pool
of a tree
soft flow of dancer slowing air
O dream of tree
you dream of me
O branch of itself you are a synapse
of that line
and think me
clear brain loops

the turning rings of yourself are of me

            our tissues cross

I always hoped you'd give me heart rings
                              in your dream

dear birch across from me we face
            the quiet pool of ourselves

                   face each other

                              return

      we

           look that way

I'm no tree except the part of me
as roots now new spring up among
the willows on the roadside shoots
of alder, cherry, maple runners, buds
grow at the sky from clay and gravel
daily now, each day a fraction
of the snow melts up the bank
those green plum eyes seep out.

I imagine it
a memory tree
birds in my hair
snow on the ground
the history of trees
or rocks of granite
spruce and birds
up here
the wind.

It wasn't apple
    that was cherry

branches hanging
    in the window frame

apple pasture
    cherry chickens

HAMILL'S LAST STAND (for Gladys McLeod

Our concern is tree-murder, harvest

of the forest (she's worried

they call it "timber") timber sale A04292

structure wood

could be a rough political situation,
could be

we speak as trees, innocent understanding
of ourselves

as things or places too, maybe farming
but for the mess

left on the smouldering hillsides
and silting the creeks

maybe a new crop another lifetime, no care

for the names Hemlock, Balsam, Spruce

undone words from our own mouths,
no flowers anymore but

cubic feet seven million two hundred
and thirty-eight

thousand Cedar, Larch, White Bark Pine,
trunk roots and

limbs scrapped trash-wood fuel
for the bush-fires dirty

orange summer skyline, Lodgepole,
White Pine, Other

Species, in other words

strip it, all the growth

for structure wood

core of our eyes to see and say it,
won't be taken

care of, hearts lost in the language
of public auction

only "profit" in the names, no talk
left about it, so set now

there is no argument, choices gone,
nothing left to say

Forest Ranger.

2

house of structure wood all leaky
roof this morning in the rain

sits in the chimney flashing seeps
through to the roof joists and drips

still upright tree wood (branches?)
from the floor sill to cross-beams

what cells left without the bark, root-
less timbers stand in the doorways

and window frames its ok the house
is "appropriate", our real needs

do not profit us, the hillside trees
also leak the rain down to their roots.

3

I admit the industry of it, hot
summer work, sweat and mosquitoes
in the headband of the hardhat, chain-oil,
whine of the diesel among the spruce
ehrrrrehrrr of the saw
to the heart-wood, I admit

the hi-baller works for a new pickup
each year, weekends in town
I admit his skill, I admit that he makes
a life of his own from it, with a grip
on the throttle lever, admit it

4

Probably the trees are warming in the sun
the mud dries up and hardens on the roads
streams are full and muddy now in runoff
a whole forest stretches out the new rings
probably it all just stands there, amazed
with the steam rising up from clay banks
gravel shoulders glisten
                    in the morning light
bridge planks shed roofs ditches a contour
part of a scene, probable and amazing
for the sun, warmer now towards the end
of March, a forest moves towards the light.

AMONG

The delight of making inner
an outer world for me
is when I tree myself
and my slight voice screams glee to him
now preparing his craft for the Bifrost
Kerykeion he said, the shore
now a cold March mist moves
down through the cow pasture
out of the trees
among, among

BIRD

Where the wind whines
I wind with my eyes
through the cedar crowns

feather boughs flutter
in my mind I imagine
the quiet middle air

I remember the forest now
dry leaves on the path
or was there no path

so much goes on now
except I touch the silence
floating through it still

NOTE

Mike I look through the spruce boughs
Far out over the valley
Into sun-in-the-clouds.

And I pivot, Mike
At the turn of winter
I try to be the place,
Tilt my gaze as
                    tree-face
Cedar-head
              sunshine(?)

P.S.

Now no move of any-eyes

        a winter a heavy curtain

                everywhere new snow

            all views every thing

Think spruce-face ice

            upright?

O.K.

        very far in very

            out

The cones are down
bunched
near the bottom of the fruit
sharp-scaled and bird-beaked
three-needle clusters
thin out
to the tip
transparency lying
under finger skin
conifer
iferous
condition

HERMES IN THE TREES

World word alive
in the heart circle of the moon
round and square
the trees hum and whistle
the trees bend slightly
the wind is warm and it moves
as May 1st has today
the warm spring advances
the tops of them crown in the air that moves
(can their own roots know any of it?)
O word of the world
round and square
give me such graces
and all accomplishment incline to me
the blackness and swift flight
roots held in the dark soil
bright branches to the sun and air
in other words the eye of heaven
consumed by necessity and by its redness
out through the west wall to my right
out there in the trees
as a bird rushes to perch in the moon's limb
and such a whiteness heard
that servant and messenger of the inner world
"the lightning flash
that connects heaven and earth"

out there in the gulley
the cedar-head that needs
the cedar-feet out there which wants
ever to return
twin-twisted kerkeion
the warm and dark
the roots as claws
under all of this
moving over
under

Cedar perfume forest
sunlight sweet
so silent, paths
ahead our eyes
reach out behind
to pull it all
and move it in
let it
see itself happen
quiet sweet
a sunlight forest
cedar noses perfume
burns into the closeness

A pasture full of apple trees
besides a picture of the World-Tree
full of apples. Underspring
down to the roots, sweet April
waters flowing from the cow-
dung hill into my soul a liquid
that, and full of apples
as it goes.

the plan of a tree
a system, squares
circles, rectangles
angles, all round
spaces, roads, ways
centres, the plan
of a tree
                spread out
the mind of the plant
growing out of the earth
becomes a hole
in the picturehead
at the boundaries
it becomes an illuminated hole
from every direction of the wind
now it seems larger
the spread is the gate of earth
lighted by the luminescence of its plan
the system of itself
is larger by the picture of it
and by the winds of space
pathways through the branches
its only part of the plan
yet a part
and looms out
from the middle of a place
part of itself
now part of
                    any

"The inward truth of the blood and the heart make so much greater a demand than all else - one has to wonder at <u>anything</u> else"

Duncan McNaughton

white birch
red apples
still
        trees

blood and sap
a trail
a thing
goes

a field full
the lovely
anything

ok then Duncan

child
a marriage
warm cow
hair
on our heads

ok Duncan

then "The inward
blood of the wonder
and the heart
make so much greater
an anything-
one has to demand
<u>all</u> truth."

hillsides
kids or apples
sap
    (think of it
flows

HAVOC NATION

How the earth
dangles
eyeing over the geographical heap
now the nation smothers
lays onto the private magic state
its own fake imagination.
                                        Backoff
into my own feet
and onto my own weight
leap
      and into her hair
Love tangles, in her eyes
Havoc sleeps.
                        "Cry Havoc"
and slip out the dogs of war.
The first woman will always be
the first woman and that
is a revelation.
                            How do you tell
someone else where you live? Can you
reveal it as real a place
as they sometimes think you are?

In the mountains near here
there is a woman who is also crow.
She is overjoyed with tears
when she meets another likewise crow.
Even if you knew this
could you look her up?

I also know a man who is a tree
and he received a letter
from a friend back east which ends
"It must be a very real world where you are.
Love, George"
That man is me
as well a revelation.

Well dangle then
the revelation
revolution nation
let slip the dogs of war
out your back door
Trees and Crows
are the ones what knows
this Havoc old Hav Ok
will stuff it in your Cry
this magic leaping tree
will never be the apple
of anyone else's Eye.

Out here
crystal eyes
only the snow
make it a gaping mouth
flesh and bark
make it a stem then
skin
a smooth white hide
touch to the frost bite
make it a finger
branch spread
canals for warm blood
steam in the cold air
make it a heart then
a heart ring
good wood
with a deep breath
for the star nights
shine in the moonlight
snow
up to the knees
hoof to the spring ground
heat for that foot touch

our heads move
only to see it all
shimmer in each of us
there are so many
who move through
we bump and touch
that's soft
warm
that's love
sweet birch out here
under all this winter
make it a body then
under under
its only a weight
light snow
well
its everything
all of it
all under
so we look up for it
falling over us
into the core
cover
covers us

On the earth
        <u>namarupa</u>
and In the world
        <u>arupa</u>
among the trees among
the distant lights & stars
a song
         one endless breath
each single soul of us
hearts legs eyes
flow & shine
               <u>eka</u>
early one morning
one man sets forth
through all of it
         himself, the mountains, creeks
& many other creatures
anywhere

this is a hard language to work out
the images keep interupting the talking
trees keep being pictures of themselves
my words keep meaning pictures
of words meaning tree
and its not easy
to find myself in the picture
except there is a strange familiarity
I remember something which is not a dream
and surely it isn't only in the mind
when I step out into the forest
even think it
not before
there is a distinct signal
of a condition or presence
I and the trees are there
in tune with it
call it a quietness
I see trees around me
or I am looking at a tree
the actual shape of such appearances
are home
and I fall into them in a flash
I recognize it now as Love
that's what goes on

Biography: It started between Mike and I just after I moved out to South Slocan from Buffalo. Then Stan started listening to them when he came up from Vancouver. Last fall Derryll said he and Michael would like to print them on their new press up in Argenta. So a week ago Gladys and Lars arrived at South Slocan and so did Derryll and Shirley. Derryll said he was ready to print, so. Brian arrived Monday night and he and I came up to Argenta Tuesday. We ordered the paper that afternoon. Wednesday morning I talked with Bird about doing some drawings for the book and so that started then. Gladys M. also arrived on Wednesday to work on her magazine, Hamill's Last Stand. Brian gave a reading that night and I started working on the typewriter Shirley had found for us over in Meadow Creek. Yesterday I talked about Love in the World Problems class in the Argenta Friends School and started typing plates. Today, Pauline, Jenefer, Erika, Gladys and Lars arrived. Michael and Derryll are up the hill printing. Bird is working on the title-page drawing. The house is full and the sun's coming out over the head of Kootenay Lake. It's 4:30 and that's about it.

April 28, 1972

Four hundred copies printed at the Root
Cellar Press for the Vancouver Community
Press.

(FROM)

Among

(1972)

Hey Dad

The Shore

Oh Dad

The Shore

FOR THE WESTERN GATE

It's hard to believe
Enough of this to make
The horizontal land appear
A place or highway
Here or in the starry sky
And trust my eyes to speak.

The sky was there last night
There above the dark range
Clear over the mist and trees
That star, she said, is that
The look it sees us through?

Hard enough to see
One small point or passage
And take that the Gate
The byway and a password
Now to know I go as I look
Not otherwise only
Through the mouth of eyes
I speak for myself I
Want to go out there out
Over the view to look for

THE CANOE, TOO

there is all that talk about northern waters
lakes with canoes sliding silently over their cold glass surfaces
    in the moonlight
and a mountain rising to the moon in its ice and snow
the rocky shore and its cold dry branches of driftwood waiting
for you to return alone in the still night
shimmering darkness

there is all that talk of this
and the mind wanders there in a canoe language carries
like a picture framing you in the black ice water

there is all this kind of talk and you listen to the words

the northern lakes freeze
over the ice snow covers the valley
    and all the trees

FURS

for Jack Clarke

I

Fur
is the woods
fur
the soft bound ball
body slat (down at the river
laid out in
fur
the dead dog the dead fur stiff stuff
corpse
1846
"it was no longer profitable to trap the beaver"
1834
1820 1821
in a dog's yelp
beaver
horses
tracks on the earth
but not beaver
dogs
are our fur's the same thing
the same reach
for beaver
and rivers
go where
the men go those trappers those lyrical
trappers
song-minded americans
in dog's yelping
to Astor
sittin' in new Yawrk
sippin' gin &
beavers and boats around the continent
not fur
not where
the missouri is not a starting place where
the beaver is
is

(they no longer have any names those thompson simpson men's
journals crossing the continent by water by portage by grease
pemmican & tallow, the fats the meats made possible the "inland"
voyages to the sea (and beaver?) the columbia and down the wide land to
portland and back up the interior to the trails and furs)

spreading
those pierced-nosed ones
ponies
bickering posts
it was not for money
it was for men
and their fur
was "land"
geo-
fur
is the overland is the river the portage

where I sit up on a deer bear run
no longer a trapper's trail
and think that I have discovered
a language in the warm afternoon breeze
inside myself I feel the kootenay to issue
from out of
as vapours
and the clouds which shuttle the mountains' peaks

where the beaver builds
he moves up to the head
at the back of the place
and makes that the place the water comes out of
before the flow
begins
there the beaver builds
a bridge of mud and birch
and then the creeks below
No – anywhere he can do it he does
anywhere
build a creek song
build something
but that fur is in warmth
like a lie

II

rubaboo
the murky soup
somewhere
a mix-up
the incline of
Howser Ck.
to Taurus Mt.
four squatters that way
Starbird Glacier on the right
nine cabins
two and a half decades of winters
muskrat martin
Hans Rasmussen
his my snowshoes
look
with an eighty-pound pack
go with his eyes look
what else can ya do but
stare the bear down
and on and on
his politics
the eyes of absolute necessity

III

the fur
is as clear as can be had
as transcontinental
or men of which virtue
they occupy little space
in a canoe
not fur
at all

in Buffalo – May 1966

IV

In the Winter of November 1969

(Going now to where this came from
only to arrest the world as a going-on
"experience of earth" and my friend from Chicago
says "walk right through all that"

November 14, Apollo 12
has just been struck by lightning
and above the Kootenay River
the affirmation of strength and "infinite possibility"
straight out the front door
the very fur Thompson's men didn't
or even Loki
stretched out under the apple tree sleeping
as I a joy
step on this morning
the lip
to hold all of it there
a magnet
that dog's eyes
the obvious
farnesses)

FOREST

And we just stood there
in the Forest
look
at everything around us
looking
surrounding

ALL EYES

for Jenefer

She is as yet
all eyes to see
and must look out
at everyone

(from on her back
the leaves
the falling green
of trees fall to

her eyes o eyes
her aye well-seeming
eyes.

THE FLOWER

The Mountain sits
in the men's minds
of the east

flowering
as some white
and green lip
or petal

in the imagination
of colours
and size

fragrances and ice
a timberline
scree, some grass
lake and rocky
streams

all
in their imaginations
that it is a mountain
they sit upon
crying out up the valley
"A Flower, a Flower!"

THE LEVEL

In a mind of mountains
the topography is cocked for disguise
the heart expects
everything moves as a level
surprise trips and turns the eye
the big boot starts in the underbrush
so readily stupidly
to follow the mind
which is tricked. What stick
but a fresh-barked log wet
can start the foot slip lose
the elevation of the line a
cliff creek stop
what the compass-eye intended?

What earth can so undermine
as well as gravelly roots
your ass in the air? Nothing
so much as the mind's line
the map to make the mountains'
trees the roads locate the eye's
desire to hold
the mirrored compass
to the eye to sight
the button push record the crown of larch
or branch or bark or granite rock.

In the mountain's mind
in the forest
there is no mistrust
the intention
of the topography
to be true
is as much a level
of the heart
as lines to place
a map the mind locate.

LETTER, OCTOBER 18/67

this morning there was snow
as far down as our house
thus the hills were covered
and into the valley below
just wet puffs dear george
dear jack dear women &
hung on the spruce boughs
bent the bushes' branches
onto the picture of the road
and me driving through them
the road beneath our house
the old highway I come off
our steep dirt driveway onto
and you know how excited I get
about snow and jennefer too
pauline never gets excited
dear mike already written
dear pat please come & see us
the river I drive along every
morning its steams rise
you know a recurrent picture
of all I know of Würm
glaciation dear jack here is
a very good map of the arctic
for on it you can see
Franklin's men & all their
Lime juice the Ag-loo-ka
(Crozier) was the Esh-e-mit-ta
& particularly Crozier who comes
out of the wind of snow & mist
only when that is what you want
to know will then be imaged
for you and also it is a good map
for Thos. Simpson, Point Turnagain
and death how does the war look
from there this year it looks
more like a mouth from here
in the mountains where the snow
has come lower daily from the peaks
and now on the apples pauline still
hasn't picked outside our kitchen

– ahh I don't know I miss you all
and that going to "started and went
toward Oot-koo-ish-ee-lee (Great
Fish or Back's River), saying
they were going there on their way
home." cold snow

ALL THAT WINTER THERE

We are gone outside
you and I
through our door into the cold night
that is like icicles between us.

Your face is white also
as the powder snow
out there behind our faces.

A complete cold lies all about us
now the door and cold air
the stare between us freezes
then you walk outside alone
on your own white snow into
all   that   winter   there.

THE SNOW STARS ROCK

Yah it's a picture
the green boughs bow
the snow down
the black night fills
the top branch the treetops
it's a picture the world is
thrown down snow castles
from the night above the snow
above is filled with stars
are filled-in warriors
and dog heroes
                                        quiet now

the hillside
sidles up as I
up the sky I move through

        the trees   white moon
        O hang on   hang on
        the rock clear dark fir boughs
        dark wet fir-boughy roads

        in the silences and under your blazing timber sun

down
the mountain
four feet above your silken grass sides the bark flies from
the pitch sticks

        yes mud
        yes please hang on
        propulsioned sights

                        uh-huh a picture
                        I is eyes in the stars
                        I look at I be
                        a ceiling of soft   dark
                        height...

THE HILL THE RHYTHM MOVES

truck the tires black rock-pocked rubber gravel dust
the road

the road it is on (length) the side (where)
west
move over it (the road) the slope slopes

a way in an edge it is
the growth cut
away the right-of-way
wynds

into the shape the sidehill is
an "up"
at the round of my back behind
down behind before where I was

the creek up
the hill beside
the road by
under me

there on the top in the mountain at the trees blue sky green light

at noon (then) the logs marked (volume) by us (thirst)

turn and take under the road legs and the creek beside down to the lake
and highway
at the mouth
shore
the colour in the water is the trees'
blue sky green light from the hills up

UP THAT HILL & INTO THE TREES

you bastard
and don't stop –

run
a turn is a trunk
the bark the coat of
a stem that I am
a sapling it is
into brush into
needles my eyes
the head in the green
of its branches
the rough it is
rough to the face
my bark is hit
hair in the pitch
stick in the crotch
scrape against bark
open the skin
from the eyes in
the needles the
needles the green-blue
through the bunches
its shoulders feet
caught betwixt roots
twist the boughs
who give way they
bend the pitch stays
the air a shimmering
sunlit haze of pollen
I'm into the trees
my legs the hill
                                        is.

(a ship
sails by with a face
and a flag
I want to be the flag
up there
and a moon
in a dark and tossing sea
let me be the tossing
no I'll be the road
over the hill and out of sight)

THE DECLINATION OF THE COMPASS NEEDLE

in 1957 is decreasing 3.8 minutes annually in 1963
it is not from Mount Christine what
little difference a new poetics/topographics

yellow
ribbons
plastic yellow
ribbons

just the mark
and twist of number

only streaks in the trees
to measure the image

like any point
the needle.

POEM FOR TURNING

Move down zigzag
through switchback
through sideways
move down there
move side right
move left
keep right angles
head front-wise
cleft earth hold
the fall line
fall to trees
keep incline
be degrees
go corner
move side move
jut out

in boots road pickup sidewise wide three ruts
wheel ridge grass switch eyes move in boots

in
heel
knee
cut sidehill
ditch runoff
move down
ricochet track
line shove
spin out fall
back fall side
saw the forest
clear the creek rock
split the sky
open roll dig
cover burn
fill the fill
and cross the bridge
turn up
turn into turn
at it

NEW HEAVEN & EARTH

I point to my own absolute (?) experience of
myself as a step towards which all
my being flows (into) & fills and from that there
a physical place out of which the possible

---

so

rete

the inner joyous heat

which earths it through me

then

Of all at this here

From the hill

To Me

the place of myself

CAULDRON

...above all upper Bonnington

... so much as there is a steady flow of breath
of him who is the turbine of his own sources
it comes from the base of the neck
from a small hint of light far back of what is about to happen

SONG

What a wonderful way
To come into the city
All over the bridge

O
        ver
                  the bridge.

TRIP

I knew where I was
and I knew where
He was

cuz I took Him there.

O yes I did.
it's what He wanted
weren't it?

APPLE

His Idea
of (Car) Beauty
in His Eye
(Raspberry)

Hers of Travelling

Lemon (Maybe)

Apple
in Their Heads.

A MISSILE

O Jack
    what a relief
a laugh
    this morning

see everything goes anywhere
that any other place
is also
      there.

Believe me
    it is pure joy
to overshoot the moon
and find you
out there
      too.

REPORT

Jack I went up Main Street
the ship
of your big white convertible
tracking

curtains sliding
candles for head sockets

heaves within heaves of her flow
and tears at the edge of

she spoke of you
I did we circled
on you like that
then it was hours
the beer loosened
talk fell back to
her eyes cushioned
in on themselves

in on the storm.

MANLY ROAD WATERMELON BLENDER

          red rhubarb
play the box
          so say what yOu want
                    and yOu can care for me tonight
          to play this box
                    you make it
with a box
    a box
        a picture
                baby Mary
    meadows are
        so Baby
blue and green
    why don't you go the way
        red rhubarb does
                ech
                red rhubarb
        break his heart
    and break my heart
you've been promised a lid
        a heaven
            oNo

GOODBYE THEN

So
what was that you said
that night what the last
time in the morning out
side his Volkswagen there
the very last time in
that place you know that
humid city what was it
on that street (a wedding
yes later in the day) then
but who was it blew
the night that most last
coloured hour on the stage
the jazz in all our drinks
some final word that dawn's
look Michael Jack Mary Bob
Pat what was that you said
then
        on Brewster Street
        in Buffalo 14214
        New York?

Wallow
in our souls?
You crazy Canadian
you American you
any of you show me
how large love will be
or far, the sound of him
entering his chariot. What?
You wallow in your noises, cut off
distances the magnitude
of such brilliance you will not allow
or carry above yourself
the sound of the gate of his chariot
is air
any one one of us shines
any two of us beacons
how far off into it
is the only definition of the size of
anything, call it something like a butterfly
you crazy people
is possible.

COVER

this
is the enchanted forest this
is Criseyde and Gawain in the rain this
is too important it is dark
out under the trees
          there is too much going on
                    out there
          the stars
                   are there
              the fog is
there it's cold the stones
are wet and slippery

the woodshed is out there somewhere
they are screwing up their lives
in the castle the feast is very important
the kisses are the war was
the hunt is every day away all day
the grass is shiny
         here is the moon and
            here is his shield
                    his horse
                                  carries a ton here
is the axe
              there
       is the forest
where is her palace now
                why is she here
                                         look
at his heart
where has she gone and why
is he sleeping in the rain
            this
is really the enchanted forest
            her picture
is on the cover

HERE

is a dead letter, Mike
the postal gods there
are warring
and the neighbours, they
spin
get out in their cars
rubber
in our backyards our parking lots our
garbage cans
the noises
are everywhere
is there a war on
there is such a storm
for the cars, where will they
all go to
our neighbours
on such a tempestuous night
a night
Wait!
There she is
see her, on the corner
thin wristed twirling her waist
amulets tinkling, O god
her earrings
laughing

LETTER, MAY 15/68

Mike, the Hang-up Is Her

river revere
power magic
hums high away
flowers out valley V
O river my girl
the doll of the valley
kiss dance
they drum
they give out many things
& another is kissed
she is given multiple items
her drum is many
it pounds out ready
koot-nay-eee
her bum in the air
tits to the moon
road runneth ever
it flows
pounds giveaways
very late
very dark at night
her kisses are many things
mysterious steering
her dance is as her drum is
many kisses / much river

A POSSESSION IN GREAT MEASURE

for Jaquie

I

That shape of this in me
the sudden presence of your eyes
a world I want to call not Love but clearly
lovely water shining
from your clear shining water.

II

Illuminate
a world then?
Show through
the many brightnesses you offer mine
to give away so easily a possibility
I mean the miles and minds you've covered for me
and didn't mean to, well
you did, you
gave to me
what was it?
A morning moon and sun, then
a valley full of tired, tired talk
that soft the endless layers
that soft and well your chiding leading
where can anyone shine through, so
light a place for all of us
except with you
but what you are a possible
an eyelight
then.

III

I'll take your tears also
as a gift
they are the shape of brilliant seas and fears
the deepnesses
you show and give to me
the clear night.

Now I tell you that I wanted them
something necessary
like the ferry
over shining water
something like
a river.

THE ADVANTAGE OF YOU

Here
let me, only
occur it
for myself
anyway

When I was a child
and then later
a whole generation

... it gets complicated

somehow
the story
I find me in
too

e.g., I know this girl
who grew all this corn
and called herself
the "tassel girl"

She
even planned a party
to illustrate
her edge

BORNING

Do you two know
in your round eyes
that what you share by them
shines clearer now
than breaking water?

Show me that world
you both acknowledge
by your looks
is only yours.

What is that thin shoreline
between you?
Beach and water
a container
of continuing birth
and feeling?

Let me see it
every day Pauline
and Jenefer.

... WITH FEELING

Build a big
uh ... anything

"Like a, like a
drum, a drum"

And hit it now
all over town, you

Show 'em spin
their heads

And How
to make a bang

A Great big
noise of yourself.

RECOVERY OF THE MIND

Vancouver turning on
straight off Great Lakes'
humidity I thought, rather
observed the most astounding
message to shock the inner-city wires
was from Stan and that was neither divine
nor vulgar but was what else was happening
at another level likening itself a heat wave
to the metaphysics going on up front
from Prynne and/or Dorn but bearing more the mode
of exclamation than a question like "get yr ass
in gear" he said "where are you?"
and that was as much as the limit of events
or the speed from here to there
considering the ultimate travel that any of us
is to be post-occipital looking from behind
and whispering lucidities to ourselves
it was all rather weather thunder
quite a jolt.

WHAT I MEAN

I never knew writing was this easy. All I have to do is do what I'm doing right now, like say, "I never knew writing was this easy" – just saying it. That means a lot to me cuz it means I can say just about anything I want as long as it's what I want to say. I guess it's the utter truth or honesty that is so attractive in language. The *virtu*, some say. It, for example, could go something like this:

I've thought for a long time now that *Hockey Night in Canada* would make an excellent title for a book. There's something to it that proposes all sorts of interesting possibilities of what to say. At first it was a long poem, epic perhaps, containing all the music of a hockey game, the movement over the surface of the ice, the satisfying accuracy of the puck slapped into a corner of the net, any of the action going on. Then it was to be a story of my own story, a spiritual biography containing images of my life, my father standing against the boards of the arena, both of us, watching the Swift Current Indians practise, my first skates, my first wound, anything, I felt, that could be a part of the blood. I still think it's a great title but today I just say it and you know right away that that's what I mean.

Earth

(1974)

EARTH
fred wah
curriculum of the soul
no.
6

how to live as a
single natural being
the dogmatic nature of
(order of)
experience

how many?
& how each
made known,
exercised,

as

Ismaeli muslimism

&, all together,
create
organism

organs &
function - activity
of the soul
or psyche or
Heaven or God

Alchemy - rather by plates
[as connected to dreams]
pictorialism

as in Earth, "View"

& perspective
/cf. Weyl on ocular
power

Vision

+

Messages

technically, Analytic Psychology, as only technical study I
know of modern Western man & under enough mental
control

jazz playing

dance as individual
body-power

equally say Homer's art
Bach's belief
[cf. Novalis'
"subjects"

Egyptian hieroglyphs (gesture, speech
- drawing
habits
mental condition

the Norse
& the Arabs
-locally, American
Indians

6

· EARTH ·

EARTH

•

Fred Wah

THE INSTITUTE OF FURTHER STUDIES

Cover by Guy Berard

Some of this appeared in *M.F.S.*, *Co Tinneh*, *Scree*.

This fascicle is dedicated to

Corrine Marie Erickson and Helen Deane

Mountains

Wait

Oh inward-flowing

winding hot canals and chasms of delight

undermoving light in the treetops

born on its own wind

synaptic beads and islands

stars or heart beat boulders strewn

boils at the touch.

The nutrient rock feeds

a lovely flower her blossoming

embrace.

Oh inward-moving beams

who whirl as the orb whirls.

It's a red globe not green whirling (let it whirl) out of mind and sight. Eyes and a hand or foot are required to measure the process between the shoulder blades of this burden. This is a ravine-like latitude on which rests a weight as solid as a lake, conclavity held there by foot-step and rock-ripple. Arms recognize directions the fingers hold to. The whirling motion is a thought similar to a blue sky. The fluidity of the lake, frozen or not, is a part of the size. Its all pretty close to what's going on where mind, eye and lake meet to provide name and home.

On the earth

      namarupa

and In the world

      arupa

among the trees among

the distant lights & stars

a song

       one endless breath

each single soul of us

hearts legs eyes

flow & shine

             eka

early one morning

someone sets forth

through all of it

          himself, the mountains, creeks

& many other creatures

anywhere

CRUISE

...so I told myself I would go out wandering not over the world but in the world until I found instant upon instant of that minute contact with a piece of it, say a twig, or a woman but with no other intention than an afternoon walk or a job might be in getting some work done and that at any place along the way I could dwell there forever in a state of property or it might be a more lively endeavor in which things would be counted, three switchbacks, a washout, a city, five gods, etc., i.e. I would be out there in it with everything else collecting measurements with my senses in a timeless meandering through the wonder.

1.

Heavier than air
                  on the traverse
                                   over
outward through October
movement rewired as crisp air again
                                      heavier
          oh so much caught
in the microscopic particulars of its weight
just as the padded paw-print, just so.

Now in San Francisco a poet returns
announced in two about ten-line poems on the front page of the Chronicle
something in one of them about this is where I have been
and now I am back I've been in the woods, in a creek in fact

Its morning
fallen
to the earth

the apples have had frost by now
pasture's full of em the cows'
cream becomes heavier
all
glitters
picks up the shift and twist
shift
and switch
again
and again

there's music and dancing in the fields and visions in the tall couch grass
there's nothing new in all of the strangeness of even our dreams these nights
nor of the moon coming back into the play of a renewed illustration of the tracks
contained in taste the multi-million flavours of the presence placed

simply placed
in mouth

the particle
the hue

outside the room to left or right along the beams and over the door jambs
the six directions the four gods the seven arrows the nineteenth lunar mansion
the twenty-two and the twenty-eight the complete circle moebus strip and every feast
the whole fucking multitude coming through the door at once
each
just so, just
placed by its own weight
tells it

now I am here from where I have come crossed on over in the present body like this

2.

I was in the sky above Bonnington Falls
expansive
nearly a full moon
west from Copper Mountain to Sentinel
(he's a dog
leg of the river
or ridge

We said we'd meet somewhere along the river but no one else showed up.
There was a back road
light frost on the ditch-grass.

Alone in the night and mist moving
over the roads and rock outcrops
river shining up its banks through the treetops.

Someone's back yard
empty
the wind.
Drive around the back
from Krestova to Pass Creek from Goose Creek to Rasberry Village.

No one.

The ferry doesn't cross at this time of night.
Drive up river and over the dam.

Back in the sky
float up the Kootenay to the light
there's the moon again still crossing over the night between two peaks.

I step off the ride into our own yard
move some lumber out of the frost
putter around under the trees
cedar looming from the moon.
Body tired
pissed off
no one.

3.

In the timber Tiwaz crosses over on a spruce limb

as a boat over the ocean he flows over the windfalls

bark flies from his caulked boots and he cracks the dead larch boughs in his path

so that it thunders through the days and nights above him above his shoulders

up the valleys through the great cedar stands his crossing over becomes the mountain

across the river in the enormous distance of his cruise cumulus rolls

his weight he carries with him in front of himself he pushes out he gathers

the whole horizon his eyes sight by peaks the straightest intention of his direction

over which he disappears a gap an arc a glint of light.

In the afterwarmth

the mountains across the river shine as the mist thins

morning shows   morning shows

4.

"CHAIN"

The greatest Objects of Nature are, methinks, the most pleasing to behold; and next to the Great Concave of the Heavens, and those boundless Regions where the Stars inhabit, there is nothing that I look upon with more Pleasure than the wide sea and the Mountains of the Earth. There is something august and stately in the Air of these things, that inspires the Mind with great Thoughts and Passions; we do naturally, upon such Occasions, think of God and his Greatness: And whatsoever hath but the Shadow and Appearance of INFINITE, as all Things have that are too big for our Comprehension, they fill and overbear the Mind with their Excess, and cast it into a pleasing kind of Stupor and Admiration.

Thos. Burnet, *The Sacred Theory of the Earth*

1.
The idea of it. Pictures form and the topography gets carried around in a head. Sometimes the feet find out what a trick the mind is. A necessary disguise for what the heart expects. But the Abney Rule and Compass are equivalently off. And so we move in on the new territory only to trip and fall over our imaginations, get lost.

2.
Snowed a few inches last night. Went up to the Giant's Kneecap - freezing wind snow and whiteout at the top. Skied down into Joker Creek a ways before we realized we were in the wrong valley.

3.
There are times moving through the bush so fast I fade into everything around me. Zigzag, switchback and sidehill force a fadeout between body and earth. Such a dance. Touch is some thing itself. A flash.

4.
Everything's out there larger elsewhere and then I add myself who's watching.

5.
Via the car journeying over the surface is when its flat. Maybe boats on still water too or skiing across the frozen lake. By plane its always there and back so more a line.

6.
Look out of the cave-mouth at an arched horizon, cut-off sky and alabaster rock wall limits. We see a night sky, the arch of stars, some heaven.

7.
The size of a river = its original ridges.

8.
We moved over the tables making our various tests for identification - hardness, specific gravity, streak, etc. Just as though we were about to cook and eat it all talk shifts to a rumour of serpentine on True Blood Mountain.

9.
Lyles Adopola. Sweet smelling orange mint.

10.
The Xthonic inhabitants of the sea, ridge-dwellers, known as 'the steady ones'.

11.
One can imagine how difficult it might be to navigate a course through some creeks, trails, and ravines which are measured both in terms of a surface (the map) and the underside of someone's idea of the place (the story).

12.
The magical alchemical inversion of it is that it is already.

13.
Duncan M. says he dearly loves his own back yard. Now I do too. The only test we have for it is the unavoidable picture.

14.
High in the mountains, high on a mountain, and spin. To ride this horizon of a thousand peaks and sky makes me dig my heels into the scree and ice and lean back hard, just to hold on even.

15.
Silence leads - sinking into the viscera - gently - head feels lighter and drained - a thin, fragile wire open now - mind of all the air surrounds me - arms and shoulders fall relaxed - carefully and softly my body is lifted back up refreshed and presented to the food - mouth holds to the first taste which fills my head stretched out now over the lake and the day.

16.
I get scared sometimes when I'm alone in the bush, especially at dusk when the stumps and rocks become grizzly bears. Never handled that aloneness, passage to becoming all one over extended time in unknown strange surroundings except to squint, peer, grope and fumble.

17.
I was sick, very sick. And I hoped for deep sleep. It seemed to me that the bed was in an east-west axis and should be lying north-south. But true or magnetic north I did not know. A cow elk appeared to me, in a valley, so I checked my compass and headed north.

severance spring water
wasp or hornet who cares
it was a toxic arrow full of information of Another World a stream of itself
immense ejaculation knockout zapping nerve box
synapse blackout another place so beautiful Pauline that's where I am
Pauline
No   No Here   uh yes   Here   I uh
slapped me back to bathroom pain and muscle struggle I was gone there
taken over
some chemical creek flowed through the dream in darkness
there was nothing to look at or any others taking part
she slapped and yelled at me
I didn't want to return
it was so beautiful this textured cool caress
the spring water I splashed on my eye
Sunday morning
Sun Trees
A Loss   A Dream
Voices in the rooms outside me

He needs adrenalin
stretched out and holding on
Needles   Shapes   Stomach (the vulnerable
fix the spring get the tools
barbed wire
his foot at the nest
bango
a distance   road   cold   fear   dead weight
jaw
the viscous fluid flowing through all my body helpless now
that power the wasp informs me of
given
such a look
at the grid of action the bloodstream's also part
the sting
it signaled it was ready for and took
on the way to the hospital she said just keep breathing I hadn't even considered it.

I point to my own absolute experience of

myself as a step towards which all

my being flows (into) & fills

and from that there a physical place

out of which the possible...

...just so's there's a steady flow of breath

of him who is the turbine of his own sources

and comes from the base of the neck

from a small hint of light far back of what is about

to happen.

Here's how it works:
the vapours rise from the seas
oceans and lakes in clouds
of liquid love for earth
blow in over the land
and fall in pearls of rain
or snow thrown by the release
of its own weight downward
where the ground distils
hence rivers flow and creeks
gush out some total soul.

Each single soul of us named Earth
put our feet on the ground and spring up
trees and little children reach
water as the geogonous fungi a rock
granno-diorite black stone and animals
eat and love

             the bough grass tail cone and root
sacred combination of its parts we are part of
and the sky out there to touch
all our eyes and the long arm
also of this breath-world
                          seeded
placed
piece after piece-

a black heifer browses through the snow pasture
or a trout up Koch Creek twenty miles north of here.

so

rete

  the inner joyous heat

    which earths it through me

                    then

AM OSPREY
BEAK STUFFED WITH STICKS/FISH FLESH

HORIZON WING
AM LAKE

FEATHERS' COLOUR REDUPLICATE
SYMMETRY WATER BROWN AND GREY

CLAW CRIMP ON KOKONEE
OLD TAMARACK LIMB

NECK JERK WORLD LOOK SKY
SCREECH SHIT BIRD-SHIT NEST EDGE

EEE   UHREE   REE

SONG

My eyes strain against the hillside for a movement, a shape, a flash of white-ass fur. I'm on the top of the ridge below a grove of poplar. This is pretty good. Its clearer here. A view with distance and I can see more of the bush, alder gulleys and old burns. If anywhere, there should be some sign here or in the clump of trees above; fresh elk shit (steaming still), a warm bed, fresh tracks in the snow. I stop for a smoke here, wipe the sleet off my glasses and rifle scope, sit on a log.

It begins as my own breathing, a rhythm in the chest picked up by the blood (pulse), short puffs of white steam from my mouth. In this the words come (language engraved in the air of a middle silence):

Stand Up

Stand Still

Be With me

Here

I don't look. Just a blue-white blur of air in front of me as I listen hard. Within me, carried by the breath, the words speak. They and I warm up to it and move now with a song, move nowhere, just sit there, now somewhere.

Out of the salt
tears, grass and browse
I've never seen a bison
or a parallel flaked point
in all my life
to cut the taste
I couldn't believe it
no matter who we were
cry out salt lick
eat it up.

*

I eye a herb
and flower
garden pauline
says so

put your foot
on the shovel
for a fat
red tomato.

*

Sweet baby!
Sweet baby!

Chicadeedeedee.

Walk out to the lip

        over the wet grass walk out

skin and blood eyes hands boots

                 again and again

even the eyes move as always moving lines

    circles

            of the morning sun

    curriculum

               of soul

*

wait for
the sky to come up
on the peaks' horizon
aphorous line
cloud
the blue
stars
night
a spinning
earth
day
glacier
morning star

*

anxious
to be weather
rather
be too wet

*

rained light
and concoctible
limpid sweet
and grateful
to taste thin

then rises as a sea
to a heaven
called the air

*

on the b

on the bottom of the sea

but in the green and coral

pleasurably   pleasurably

*

Eth means why any one returns
every one all over the place they are in
entwined into the confluence of the two rivers
into the edges of a genetic inscription
and our homes and loves now night
spreads out up the valleys
into the many-forgotten messages and arrangements
carried there the character sticks
hunger

Geoblast plumule

which in germination

rises from the ground

such as the peas blast forth

to the space above in time

a geochronical event to lean in

on the surrounding space

incline or cyclic revolution

spinning latent circling forces

of the earth

said to spring directly from the surface

of itself or skin the iso-

thermatic under-sperm or milky way

is language only after all

selenic moon

The reticular net or grid
we both are and see before us
in the world including heaven
as well as hell to right and left
the stages levels or lines
of force segmentative views
but no inferno flaming underground
just fixed in place before our eyes
the chance to be exposed to all the vectors
of this plan we carry everywhere
to move on and into the sensation
fear and joy or maybe apprehension
of the range of being where one is
enlarged by all three or dozen worlds
and illustrated only by the feeling
for it.

To think of it is big. Memory of having been anywhere on earth embellishes the particulars of those instants of specific step or touch and forms a living picture with all the referents of home, roots, heart, core. In earth I find an ever-luminescent atmosphere of primary sensation and life. There are forms there which reveal to me shapes of myself; pieces and names which provide aspects of an identity; tree, ocean or whatever signals as both participant and reflection. It all becomes picture, movement, body, texture and idea - images of real palaces encountered which permit the extended traverse and transport through landscape. I think earth is a condition of ourselves we all have access to.

A CURRICULUM OF THE SOUL

Vision — Drummond Hadley
Ismaeli Muslimism — Michael Bylebyl
Woman — John Wieners
Messages — James Koller
Alchemy — David Tirrell
Dance — Lewis MacAdams, Jr.
American Indians — Edgar Billowitz
Dante-Giotto — Robert Duncan
The Norse — George Butterick
The Arabs — Edward Kissam
Novalis' Subjects — Robert Dalke
The Mushroom — Albert Glover
Blake — John Clarke
Earth — Fred Wah
Attention — John Temple
Bach's Belief — Robin Blaser
Egyptian Hieroglyphs — Edward Sanders
Dream — Duncan McNaughton
Phenomenological — Robert Hogg
Perspective — Daniel Zimmerman
Jazz Playing — Harvey Brown
Analytic Psychology — Gerrit Lansing
Mind — Robert Creeley
Organism — Michael McClure
Matter — John Thorpe
Homer's Art — Colin Stuart
Sensation — Anselm Hollo
Language — Edward Dorn

matter

Phenomenological

Sensation and Attention
training in exhaustion &
completion

A Plan for a Curriculum of the Soul

(Intuition
& Feeling
one's own
the Mushroom | dream woman | mind language

Earth as a
geology comprehension like archeology
geography - equally, though here maps & experience of
human history walking
in this connection, as habitat
inhabitation of, rather than as politics say
or national. Instead, physical, &
vertically incremental

physical
man as animal praxis of - as Earth as a

emotional mental experience

Poets as such, that is disciplined lives not
history or for any "art" reasons example,

Blake
the same, say, medicine men

& like theologians: example, Dante - Giotto

Charles Olson

the institute of further studies

box 482 canton, new york 13617

Pictograms from the Interior of B.C.

(1975)

Not the qualities merely, but the root of the qualities is trans-created. How else could it be a birth, – a creation?

Samuel Taylor Coleridge, *Literary Remains*

Under and over
I see myself rocking
boat/cradle
cave to swim into
over and over again
home again
home
again and again

What if there was a circle
and the circle was a lake
and all around the lake the stone
grew up the mountainside

but instead of surrounding
the circle was a vector of aquamarine
and rather than go round it, by turns
each of us would go into and therefore through it.

See the arrow?
Even the beetles go.
And the birds, birds
something equal or familiar
twice, a two
such as a man and a lake
a place, the place
to come back to.

On my way to get a pail of water
which way
down by the creek
down by the dark
and in the trees the night
buhdum, buhdum
bdum, bdum, bdum

oh there is no need to be small not for
anything in the world take it from anyone
on the hill don't be pushed say it first
move right at it so that you are in it
right from the start go ahead

The feathers of my mind increase
as I reach for the choices
chance for what else
other than what I knew (know)
another talks to me (I think)
something (things) to see

Hey! It Looks like
you got a couple ways in there

and a face, me
no face.

Show me how you do it
and I'll come too.

If I could have jumped over there further
just as he wishes he could have
we would both be over there smaller
and back here even more beautiful bigger
but now see that we couldn't have having crossed over.

There is the spinner
throwing out baited hooks
& tossing around dreams
visions, painted plans
hence instruction
to he-who-could-care
who runs off in a circle
telling anyone
who will listen
and soon everybody knows
but by then how much
doesn't matter
they're caught like fish
in a creek trap
entranced by the beauty
and the enumeration
of ideas
worn as feathers
around the mind
and without name
only fluff in the air
above the head

ol′ moose inside ski-doo-type world
sliding down the milky way

jumped over

the moon the house elk muskrat & beaver

all runs away runs away

over & over

& over & over

again & again

Turtle Baby

Canoe portage

How does she know that
How does she do all that walking
through the forest
How does she know the bears won't get her?

Ooh! It's a pumpkin
seed within seed
face to face-mask
twin thought, light
behind the eyes.

How does the jazz go?
Autumn moon a bit drunk
in the treetops with Wind
(north) and Pacific cloud banks
about 1959 not quite
jamming it but from here
to the coast one big
triple high C and wetter
than a duck's ass just
a sliver of a harvest moon.

September spawn
fish weirs everywhere
all through the narrows.

Upstream, upstream.

A feast for all of us
cousins and old friends
everybody dancing
like crazy, eh?

Northeast

(from family, a few friends)

I turned

since I had accompanied my father

that far

what was in the world around here

became larger

some part of it

then all of it

There's a picture up Dog Creek
of a hullabaloo.
The basalt face remembers the event
with the insignia of a chickadee
and a constipated ant
who illustrated for an entire family
the dangers of a mountain lion
waiting down the path for dinner
so they didn't.

Caribou Point
strange map
movement
forks
forks with handles
birds
pitchforks
crossed sticks
travois
thus horse
a quarter moon
a count
lonely
animal eyes

See those animals
I think moose browsing
just across the lake.

Two of us'll put on grass
thin out three to the north end
and we'll get them there like this.

uvular   moist   call
movable   celestial
and crystal clear
by the height
palatial sound
aspiral noises or
udder milk

beautiful
big
surfacing
lake

old grey white sturgeon
everything for bait

sticks
traps
gaff hooks

bloody big
beautiful belly
full fish
flesh

I walked into a battle
with the forest
I tried on the buffalo-horn headdress
things happened to me
visions and pictures
two or three signs

I pushed one way
and I pushed another way

size gave dance to me
the deer showed me form

the larval, it
opens up.

Only three persons and a dog survived
and one man
had the entire map of himself
shot out
others also
lost what had been gained
the winners were heroes
thinking more to win over
than could ever be remembered.
Remember?

nv s ble
tr ck

Birds, plants, animals
a dream of myself as whole
parts of a body
wings outstretched
a rainbow and a father.

Lost

amidst *Caloplaca*

and rising

as a bubble

from earth to sky

Moss
and the spring bloom of Peacock
or Shooting Star
Granite walls
Chariot
of the Gods
it doesn't matter
manner somehow
will get us
to the hole

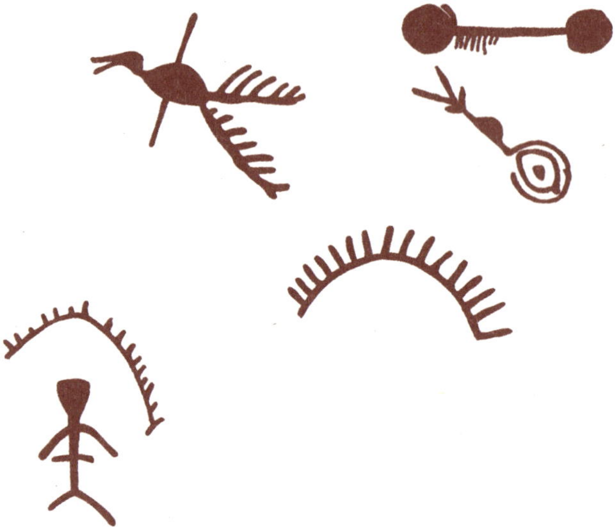

Death's stick
only
a tool
of any horizon
mountain, tree, or lake.

When they come
they come through
one way or another
or they don't get in
and stand outside wondering
but if they do
all they see are the names of me
counted out on the ochre poles.

They say one carries equally
what has been lived into death
so that I will be sheltered there
by my life. Now
it's all new to me
and not so clear
where the others have crossed.

We are different
from one another
in the space between us
a lot happens
more than of only you or I

the air
or through it all
(dog, turtle, beaver
fallen trees by the roadside
I remember)
I have come to be
no different from them

one by one one can
become the other

such as night serves
to show day's stars

Wapiti knows the way, a path
criss-crossed with events
within the roots of the flowers of vision
even inside the mountain of the idea of it
worn as horns or a headdress outside
through the trees along the lakeshore
and all over the mountains' sides
over the inside and over the outside
cover of the many, many ways Wapiti knows.

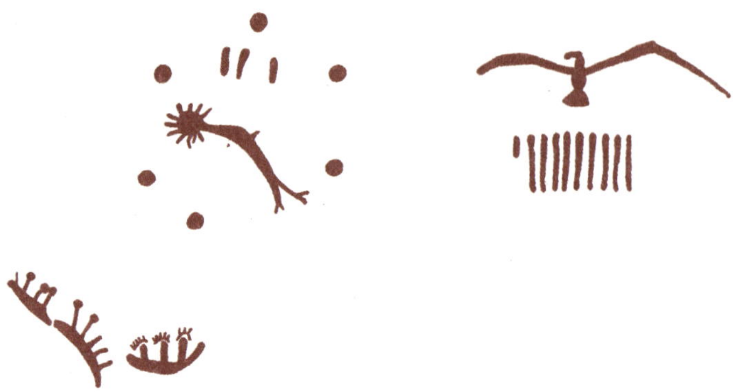

Here
this is the way
strut after strut
the blue grouse wakens stars for us
and stroke after stroke
we pass through night's constellations

that's just what the osprey sees
we say
that's right he says
we see we see.

Floating and floating
over and flying over
above or below
under and in

skein of mirror
seen as a net

the earth's and sky's
planets stars birds
flowers on the surface
of a noonday pond.

It's a place

humpbacked ant

a trap or map

foot/

the *idea* of foot

a where

a vegetable

two lakes and trees

(pine?)

five 6 seven nine and ten

it's a trap.

Ambling along
out of you
I count it all
in my mind

many many many
pretty straight
across a sky.

seagulls and a blue blue sky

seagulls' lake's sparkling waves

for other birds

                    horizon

of mountains

far from here the driftwood beaches there

trees to the shoreline

a stretch of sand

                        a place

open like this boat

antipodean

to the sky between

Another granite wall/cliff
frantic signals/reflections
        from the lake
ripple/go   (a verb
                    "to move")

here, look at this
just look at this
will you see me
("to see")

faces in my dream/directions
where the lake narrows
a full and complicated shining jewel
green, in the distance
another cliff or wall/granite

dayless

meadow of dandelion blown to seed

pasture where the lake narrows

crabgrass and sand

sunning the insides of myself / all of us

for four days frog vision

how to stand

present the body to the body

lizard   insect   fish

every day

all day

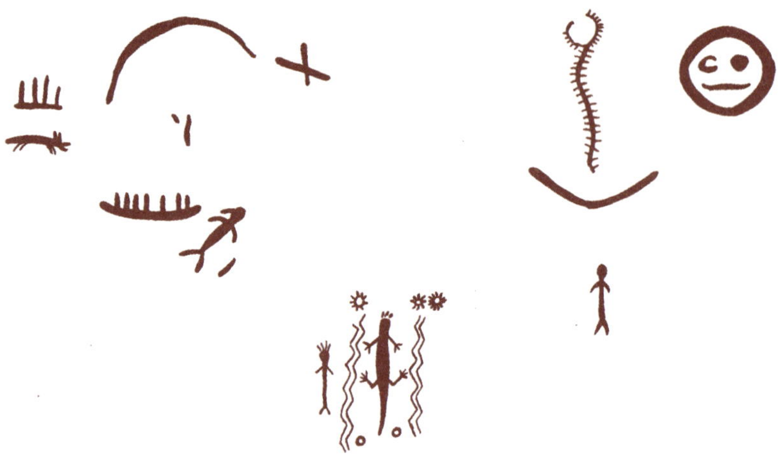

An arc

a clown (moon face in clouds)

old friends and relatives

rattling around in the boat

seen with old Peckernose our neighbour

old lizard old night to day

Count up the pure places
homes in our heads
headdress, horns to push

every time we carry
the surrounding accompaniment
(the din)

and pass forward
through the passageway
side to side

whose face, who
goes with us
how many

The wish
from what is inside
for what is out

by rope snare or spear
this is everything I figure

Heart
          Animal (arrow

what can be left

Grateful acknowledgement to John Corner, his book, *Pictographs (Indian Rock Paintings) in the Interior of British Columbia* (Vernon, 1968), from which the images accompanying these poems are taken, the work he pioneered and his generosity in sharing it. Site numbers, locations, series, and language areas are references to Mr. Corner's book.

1. Site no. 61: Mica Creek Road / Interior Salish (Okanagan)
2. Site no. 80, panel a: Pavilion Lake no. 1 / Interior Salish (Shuswap)
3. Site no. 67: Cape Horn / Interior Salish (Lakes)
4. Site no. 77, panel b: Canal Flats / Kootenay
5. Site no. 73: Redman Point / Kootenay
6. Site no. 62: Mica Creek Road / Interior Salish (Okanagan)
7. Site no. 95: Mara Lake no. 3 / Interior Salish (Shuswap)
8. Site no. 86, panel b: Adams Lake (Tshinakin Point) / Interior Salish (Shuswap)
9. Site no. 63, panel a: Christina Lake / Interior Salish (Lakes)
10. Site no. 102, fig. e1: Stuart Lake no. 2 / Athapaskan (Carrier)
11. Site no. 72: Twin Bays / Kootenay
12. Site no. 71: Twin Bays North / Kootenay
13. Site no. 76: Huscroft Mill / Kootenay
14. Site no. 6, panel a, figs. a & b: Stein River no. 2 / Interior Salish (Thompson)
15. Site no. 97, figs. g, h, k, m: Creighton Valley /Interior Salish (Shuswap)
16. Site no. 68, panel a: Procter / Kootenay
17. Site no. 74, panels a & b: Washout Creek no. 1 / Kootenay
18. Site no. 79: Dog Creek / Interior Salish (Shuswap)
19. Site no. 66: Caribou Point, Lower Arrow Lake / Interior Salish (Lakes)
20. Site no. 63, panel b: Christina Lake / Interior Salish (Lakes)
21. Site no. 78, panel b: Armstrong Bay/ Kootenay
22. Site no. 75: Washout Creek no. 2 Sturgeon / Kootenay
23. Site no. 69: Kuskonook / Kootenay
24. Site no. 77, panel a: Canal Flats / Kootenay
25. Site no. 78, panel a: Armstrong Bay / Kootenay
26. Site no. 88: Shuswap Lake no. 2 / Interior Salish (Shuswap)
27. Site no. 103: Fraser Lake no. 1 / Athapaskan (Carrier)
28. Site no. 64: Christina Lake/ Interior Salish (Lakes)
29. Site no. 1: Anderson Lake / Interior Salish (Lillooet)
30. Site no. 63, panel c: Christina Lake / Interior Salish (Lakes)
31. Site no. 60: Mica Creek Road / Interior Salish (Okanagan)
32. Site no. 65, panel a: Cayuse Creek / Interior Salish (Lakes)
33. Site no. 65, panel h: Cayuse Creek / Interior Salish (Lakes)
34. Site no. 65, panel c: Cayuse Creek / Interior Salish (Lakes)
35. Site no. 65, panel d1: Cayuse Creek / Interior Salish (Lakes)
36. Site no. 65, panel d1: Cayuse Creek / Interior Salish (Lakes)
37. Site no. 65, panel d3: Cayuse Creek / Interior Salish (Lakes)
38. Site no. 65, panel d4: Cayuse Creek / Interior Salish (Lakes)
39. Site no. 65, panel d5: Cayuse Creek / Interior Salish (Lakes)
40. Site no. 65, panel e: Cayuse Creek / Interior Salish (Lakes)
41. Site no. 65, panel f: Cayuse Creek Interior Salish (Lakes)
42. Site no. 70, panels a & b: Tye / Kootenay

Owners Manual

[1981]

HOW TO DO THIS

If you only do it once
you will remember that
so it becomes a river
more often present and gone
than done or will do

a mountain sits
think it a flower
blooms and dies
all of it
once carried is also held

fill all the space you can
just to do it
then imagine it
what a trick
once you move you can't stop
flowers mountains rivers
do dies did
done again
push mind wind
think of it somewhere
a given when
just once
you move
river stays.

HOW TO GET BACK

Help!
Half of me
everywhere I look
insides split too.

Get out of this
(mess)
see it
as symmetry
alignment
of the genetic
part of sky's
intricate order
jump up
into air
wave arms.

HOW TO READ A MAP

Side
to start from
side
city
get a vehicle/animal
check out the growth
look at the people
put your arms around
one of them
any one of them
stretch yourself
they're like old friends
a story sometimes
you tell yourself
then something else happens
now where are you
an intense map of routes
places to find again
or discover
i.e., imagine
through all that
but not there yet
the death
i.e., you noticed it
waits down the road
it's a story
everybody's running
someplace
over the hill
what they think is a hill
don't pay attention to the terrain
signs
become questions
maybe not a city
look at them
they are not birds

the signs are not other creatures
try this
the signs are projectile
have weight
just like an arrow
with feathers at one end
and you know what at the other
all-around things
the night sky filled with them
we still think they're stars
but they get in the way of the vision
the trace of thought, the line
grows across the plan
not a city
but a forest
with a big boulder
in the middle of it
the middle of the forest
there
proportion gets it together
in a dance
leaves us in a heat
and the complicated tracks remain
how to read get to
just to get there
gah Hahhh
headless moons
from here to there
incredibly difficult shapes
even languages
places
the place
the land jive
land
on the other side of the water

the soft, the hard
the softest hard
and more story
more directions
here to there, line
from mind
gets nowhere
past dying
journeying
and the returns
he called it
cute
boomerang
i.e., the truth
path flows
through a crowded cornfield
near Albuquerque
near Toronto
near Iraklion
south of here
ripe tomatoes
nothing solved
side is ...

HOW TO BE SOMETHING

Dream about it
get the head back
into the body into
remembering
skin
imprint of shape
into inside
and look at yourself
saying "mmmm"
remember
don't move
let yourself be caught
catch yourself
move
very fast
as fast as you can
as you can.

HOW TO GO SOUTH

Look at it
broken
pieces of an intention
it
something left over
in the corner
an accident
maybe
how do you know
an attempt for sure
but how do you know
something left
pieces/places
that don't fit together
but there they are
together
gathered
you don't know it
but see it
there / beside everything
else.
(they might be stars)

HOW TO HUNT

Colour it brown
think about it
ahead of time
think about it
afterwards
listen to you
how alone you are
sitting on a log
in the forest
look at it about to happen
completely in your mind
and the world
all the trees
even the sky
size
surrounds everything
did you remember
did you forget
say it
"sheh"
how heavy the task
I've tracked myself
to this log
nothing else nothing waits
get up (later
you'll get lost.

WHAT TO DO WHEN YOU GET THERE

Travel
when you get there
get into a corner or something
take the 90 degree horizon
and with what you still carry from your trip
put it together privately
to the others talk
tell each other of events since last together
what you're going to do tomorrow, etc.
laugh a little bit at the perspective
it's large
and when things rise in you like this
come to the surface with a force of their own
then let them
sit in the warmth
be in the middle of the large.

HOW TO DISAPPEAR

Fill up
go
fill up again
get smaller (in your head)
stretch
do one thing at a time
be with yourself
by yourself (stomach)
with others (lots of them)
focus
keep at it
deeply, deeply
think about it (arms & shoulders)
eye (the forehead)
could be moved easily
or else
stay right where you are.

HOW TO BUILD A FIRE

Get hungry
go around in the bush
pick up sticks
throw them over the rocks
into a pile
remember the smile of the heat
watch out for thorns and splinters
keep going until you've got enough
past the man at the mouth
and watch out
meet everyone else
with their sticks and logs
don't forget the rock
be big and orderly now
start the fire
and get the others
to bring in the crow
shout and jump around
maybe pray to something
scatter the pieces
bones and feathers
and remember what's left
emptyhead.

GUARDIAN SPIRIT

Number one
where did you get it
and then
who did it say it was
how long did it take you
to get it
where did you go
when it first appeared
what words did you speak
well, then, what sounds
oh
between you
who came first
how d'ya get your name?

HOW TO NEST

Hang out in the sky all day
fly as far as you can
until your heart flutters
comes back and leaves again
keep doing that
until frost covers the ground
count what you have left (the days)
spin around at your reflection on the lake
take air
sticks, twigs, leaves, moss
and settle into the night
awake in the world
ask yourself questions
look through the window
it's not copper
you'll have to have
answers.

HOW TO TAKE A LEAK IN THE SNOW ON A JANUARY NIGHT UP THE VALLEY

There's that boat again
through winter trees
look at it
look at it
                    ohhhh
a perfect half moon
perfectly drunk.

HOW TO CLEAN UP IN SPRING AND FALL

I IN THE SPRING

point to everything lying around
try to remember
kind of frown and shake your head
all of a sudden
there's more than there used to be
keep track of it
organize it all by counting
do a dance
a real funny dance.

II IN THE FALL

exaggerate
tell a fish story
your world is getting smaller
look at the sky full of stars or snow
get ready for that
wrap everything up
and nudge it softly into corners
but don't forget
tell a really tall tale.

HOW TO FARM

Wake up
and consider it
a serious possibility.

Look
out of the corner of your eye
at the garden and the buildings
in the morning.

Smile at yourself doing this.

The animals
jump over the fences.

HOW TO GET AWAY

Try to imagine it
far away
stand-up shape
as if it were meant to be
stone
choose a landscape
to be led along
a continent out there
shape far away
stone upright
ski there
or pretty soon
swim to it
by diving in
and sinking.

HOW TO FIND SOMETHING

Amble
not looking
you think it'll come to you
if it doesn't
thread line through your lips
in meditation
enclose it
in all you've passed by
count
break sticks at the tip
your legs are long shadows
a continuation
everything
an extension
and tied to
what it is
you look for.

WHAT ABOUT THE FUTURE

Time edits
your fortune
is complete with imagination
the telephone pole
will carry the news
over the grass
beside the highway
indicated by markers
whenever
you point
stand there
like a rock
painted
names
saves.

HOW TO BE SURE

This is really crazy
but underneath everybody doing something,
all the music going on, the chatter,
reflections of the sky, the time of the year,
standing around looking for direction (or something)
you can silently sever head from body
at the neck
silence the voice
return
to the seed
with wings and arms
planted
in trenches
dug by mothers.

HOW TO GET LOST

Later
the arrow
of hunger
points
back and back
to just tangled
memory
then stop   you
are the only
traffic
one trail
crosses another
sticks
are not
complete thoughts
when a stone says
"pick me up"
don't listen
you need to hear
something new.

When I assembled *Owners Manual* I thought I had included a poem titled "How to Get Lost." I was surprised, when the book came out, that it wasn't there. I was sure I had included it. Had Daphne Marlatt, the editor, misplaced it? Had I lost it? For years after, I wondered about it until, one day, it tumbled out of some old folders (*Faking It*, 105).

(FROM)

Loki Is Buried at Smoky Creek

(1980)

THIS SUMMER WE'RE GONNA GET A PIG
AND FENCE IT UP IN COUCH GRASS, PROBABLY
NAME IT HOG OR PORKY
FEED IT WHEAT AND CORN
GET ALL THAT GOOD PIG SHIT
AND COME TO LOVE IT LIKE A PET
PREDICTABLE THE DAY WE SLIT ITS THROAT

I'M GOING TO KEEP ON DANCING FOR THE REST OF MY LIFE

for Lewis

Sproul Plaza body writhing on the asphalt
then swaying in the bandstand, Lew
did you ever play the saxophone
in your high-school dance band
especially "'A' Train" and heft the axe
in a slight tilt till you tipped the music
and wailed out of your left shoulder
swirled honky honey blues glissandos
or maybe later used your hips
when everybody switched from jazz to Comets
you could really pull it all out
and hump your horn till you're on your knees
and the girls are screamin' and wettin' their pants
and pushing their crinolines between their legs
whew, Lew
that's what this dancer's doing on the plaza
so much into it and what you do too
so that all that Texas in your voice
sways you into the body, sways you
and us, here, Lew
read this for me will you?

IT WAS SO COLD

I COULDN'T WHISTLE

TO KEEP THE BEARS AWAY

CLOSE AND FAR

Cause yourself
move dream-power
in the midst of all others
aware yourself for their eyes
inscribe your own event for them
only keep what is not asked for
and be arrogant in your reply
that you dwell alone
on the shores of your own possible energy
at the edges of intuition and feeling

so flow yourself
a little revelation.

SUBTLE BODY
THROUGH AND THROUGH
CATCH BREATH
RUN UP TO IT
CATCH BREATH
LET IT GO
GO WITH IT
BREATHE THROUGH
FILL AND GLOW
WARM 'N MURMUR

ONE MORE ADEPT AT
STANDING UP
AS BIRD
AND SEE OUT OF BIRD-EYE LOOK
FROM TREE BRANCH
THE WORLD IN FRONT BELOW
AND ALL AROUND
NOT NECESSARILY
SINGING ANYTHING

FIRST PERSONAL POEM

You and I
(exclude everyone else
this is a physical metalogical problem

out there
grow the flowers
I could put in a vase
and leave for you

when I am not with you
I am always with you
love is a part of it
also the mind

a picture
of you
not I
nor the flowers

let's change the picture
visualize it
all, including the problem
and colour too.

JUST ASK

been there many times or at least

one, Jim Koller

and two, Paul Klee's painting

a ship sails by with a face on it

and also, three, calligraphy is beautiful

don't put it all together,

it is.

The heavy Chinese figures my father and grandfather bet on the lottery

paper of soft tissue with wet purple pencil marks time too to remember

images of Jim Koller in Oregon Wisconsin and Maine signs enough

(dogs, travel, cabins)

or better yet

> Drive .6 miles south from the main gate of the Kohler ranch. Stop
> and look over a small bank on the west side of the Richter Pass road.
> There is a rock slide on the east side of the road.
> All the pictographs are in red on a panel two feet by three feet.
> Some lichen is growing over the panel but most of the pictographs
> here are in quite good condition.
> Fig. a is located by itself at another site 100 yards southwest.
> According to Mr. H. Kohler this is a piece of what was at one time a
> huge granite boulder near the edge of the orchard.
> It has since been blasted apart and bulldozed out of the orchard area.
> As these sites are on private property,
> you must ask permission.*

next time I'll take a photograph

it doesn't matter does it what the things mean

they return to you

in the simplest and most obvious, really,

desires.

---

* John Corner, *Pictographs (Indian Rock Paintings) in the Interior of British Columbia* (Vernon, B.C.: Wayside Press, 1968), 73.

PLANT

Not until we've talked to a growing plant
sat there with it during its own all life-day
to hear, as with the whales, the music
a re-enactment of the phrase (shape)
will the information that we eat from its flesh
make sense.

Until I've spoken with you
as you speak among the others
body to body
in the screaming pitches of a sensational atmosphere
will the message, the enchantment of its reference
take root in me also.

Just as you are fixed I will come to you.
I am no less held by what I am –
you spoke first
was it only the air humming
a simple signification of presence
your presence?

Take this too, blue chicory
dandelion, cow-tree
we participate in a melody
so clear and so beautiful
I reach out to you as you do in every way to me
so we are in the body, in the body, of the song.

FROM IN HERE ...

Writing has a lot to do with "place," the spiritual and spatial localities of the writer. I see things from *where* I am, my viewpoint, and I measure and imagine a world from there. Oaxaca, Vancouver, the Kootenay River a thousand years ago or today, my father's father's birthplace, become "local" to me and compound to make up a picture of a world I am native of. Writing is sometimes remembering this image, and sometimes it has to make it up. Malcolm Lowry says he thinks of himself as "a great explorer who has discovered some extraordinary land ... but the name of the land is hell ... It is not Mexico of course but in the heart." Writers are wonderers. And wanderers. The American poet Ed Dorn reminds us that the stranger in town is interesting because he at least knows where he has come from and where he is going. Writing is sometimes useful that way, with news of the world out there. But out there is only meaningful in its correspondence to in here.

I live in the "interior" of British Columbia and such a qualification affects my particular sense of what the world looks like. We go "down" to the coast, which is the exterior, the outside, the city. The spaces between here and there are part of a vast similarity. The towns become predictable in their activities and appearances. Castlegar and Prince George, though specifically themselves, share certain aspects of distance, colour, and taste. One feels at home nearly anywhere there are rivers, pulp mills, trucks, the mysterious gravel roads further inward, and similar "local" inhabitants. Down and out there the exterior becomes more. Vancouver leads to other cities and countries, etc. But all of it, out there, is measured from in here. In the particularity of *a* place the writer finds revealed the correspondences of a whole world.

December 1976

Rooftops

(1988)

ASIA

rooftops
ridgepoles

NARA

buddha thought, buddha nature
window in the temple he looks out of

eye of heaven
roof, horizon

incense and water trough
something beautiful called hunger

the deer everywhere, us
stone lamps, words we need to know

mountain, memory
serpents, circles

bird tails on rooftops, fish in mind
everything here, everything there

DECORATION

Pots – shards – very red
horses – just a touch of legs
          highlight royalty
gold-plated fish fights for serving dish
jade and turquoise bird on top of her
          head, the border
of the house
those ends of roof beams – ceramic
face or imago imprint
rediscover a *use*
for decoration.

JIDAI MATSURI FESTIVAL OF AGES

Go to war
without animal signs?

Parade
without music?

IKEBANA

don't make it up
find it

dead brown pods
a few shiny green leaves period

HŌRYŪ-JI

we didn't see the hall of dreams
closing time, late afternoon
light dust under the branches
cool air settles around the pond

old roots, old trees, as we leave
I show my daughter
bronze serpent at the water trough
tail still coiled under wooden lid

RYŌGEN-IN

A-UN
stone words for breathing in and out
breathes in and out, in and out
shadows lengthen, someone
planes wood on the other side of the wall

beneath my feet, river stones
no river
legs dangle over the warm cedar porch board
no question

THREE HAIKU ON 37TH VIEW OF MOUNT FUJI

Nothing, but nothing
over misty fields, blue rooftops,
a few smokestacks.

Dark clouds, I think of
first quiet snow now covering
Kokanee Glacier.

A black shinkansen
tunnel out of sight, mountain
into mind's eye now.

SMELL

empty streets at dusk
suddenly an incense shop
closed

SAME POEM OF KYOTO SUNSET POLLUTION

fresh smell of burning rubber clutches *or*
burning rubber
sunset in the western hills *or* sunset
streets full now with slowly moving
headlights *or* headlights

KITANO SHRINE

clap twice
ring the bell-rope
again again
rub cowness onto yourself from the stone
clap twice and mean it

TŌDAI-JI

cathedral space, cathedral buddha
incense clouds hang around huge bronze
lotus petals
crowds silenced
by the size of the thought

TEMPLE ZOHONGUE

Dao

Caged words
fish (later, birds)
tired (tiled?) at the end
of the ridgepole

NINNA-JI

late afternoon in October
cool pine odour on the hillside air
day empties out
cedar porch board surface still warm
in the long shadows
                                        oh

KATSURA

too-perfect thought
twilight
of expectation
even this rain of intention
pond pool
path post
rough bark troughing
water not far enough away
so much itself
thinking pit-a-pat (structure wood)
be done w/ the roofs, bridges
perfect idea, trees
the empire thinks itself...
(even the carp
swim

BYŌDŌ-IN

I look out with Amitābha
through the temple window
grey sky, rain has stopped
looking, looking, looking.

At home
a light chop on the alpine lakes
a few flakes in the first winter wind.

FROM THE PLAINS OF SAGA TO NAGASAKI

Hear the scenery
out of the mountains
rice farms to the coast
Peace Park skims
the sadness

Nagasaki pointed
(not painted)
hard to locate
that lapis
in our lives

MATSUO SHRINE

Shinto simple
turtle fountain architecture
shakuhachi soft beyond the gate
tin bell bell-rope
plain paper tied to trees

STATION / TRAIN / ROOF

House barn cathedral temple and sky
Toba station to Taki
Hankyu line home tonight

AMANOHASHIDATE

heaven's bridge
horizontal bifrost
memory of each single name
hung on wood or paper
written under roof tile, copper
lucky shape for true ideas
sign to carry place or person
incense into trees outside
image remind mind

HOMETHOUGHTS

wet leaves on the ground
a roof and a house

(FROM)

So Far

(1991)

SCREE-SURE DANCING

home-truths pin-apples part fossil through fertilization flight or
eyesight could be sky or ducks fishing

•

recognize the plumes   of a Spanish kind of writing
ancestors   as certain types of Atlantic
animals   something from Anatolia   with an "im"!

•

History of the sky engenders the diverse faces of religion
All kinds of stuff like hooks and coat hangers inflate and imprint there
                                    Trace
                                            (d)

•

War on your back
Raw no-words ruin
Real Clear Nuclear

•

"Ever try to copy Texas?
All those beans, all that plastic?"

– "I can hardly keep the road plowed."

•

HERE WE EVENTUALLY ~~THERE~~ EVEN VELOCITY A TIDE SUN
(SQUINTING) CIPED PAST THE ART THE SURREALISM OREGON
JUST HELP YOURSELF CLEAN UP EGYPT AS A PLACE IN BRAZIL
BUT NO FURTHER EAST TIME AND RICE SEPTEMBER BURNT
TEST TEST

•

thoughts different
sky's all animals. all
paper. all chalk. Our

•

writing as anamorphous river cliffs	=	the tableaus of voyage forgetting

•

She danced the strict linguistic sense.
babbled bavardage   finger-painted thick
memo-clouds in the darkening sky

•

$\text{h}_{\text{om}}{}^{\text{om}}{}_{\text{e}}$

•

That's the secret
ticket
to silence
na (frame) na's notation

•

... each box of art jangles (peut-être)
a purchase on the edge of its own sequence
reflects adjacent body-language events even foreign
the container of *white* we unfortunately call history.

•

ohh   at nigh   night

Egypt

eh^{x}______ap^{i}s______apex

•

Maybe it was a dream grammar mountaining out the hypostatic river as an approximate desire but instead stretched striding or what I count on under the cedar tree down by the road for final blue prints to the heart's property.

•

cellular memory linked to sunset effect
so *sunyata* revealed as absolute closure

•

I want one ethnic thing here.
right from the start. Dis-
orientation.

•

January birds
huddle on top of chimney
Wind the letter *A*

•

Loki; you
stomach

my sound.

•

Whenever I smell the raiments of message or caprice on you I get jealous and re-invent old dance asterisks without code.*

*echoes

•

All the city
song, the great
city air.

WHAT DOES QU'APPELLE MEAN?

Did you know I watered the Japanese cherry out front?

The Manchurian plum too.

How late did Jenefer sleep on Sunday?

I talked to my mom about using the wormy cherries for wine. Tell her about the worm in the tequila.

What did Erika do at Gray Creek?

I picked two cocoon-like burls off the apricot tree.

What do you think they are?

I think we should plant more flat or sugar peas from now on.

I cooked that halibut with some veggies and the leftover burnt brown rice.

I'm trying to remember a particular and specific rotten two-by-four on the deck or a blemished shingle so I can take us there by mentioning it to you, like that piece that's soft to the touch of my foot when I turn to the left side on "slantingly flying," the one you might feel with your heel as you turn the southwest corner, leaves or weeds in your eyes.

I don't think Peter and Patty will stop here. It's thirty miles north of the Trans-Canada.

You can't swim in the lake here because of the algae.

I don't have a printer for my computer so I'm using a typewriter. There's a girl here who has an old Smith Corona portable of her mother's which is just like yours, only in better shape.

This place is full of noise because it's a band camp and there's a black Lab right outside my window howling all night every night.

When I flew over Invermere the fires were really chugging out huge pillars of smoke so you could tell the mountains were in control.

They have mosquitoes here.

Is life work?

Where is my olive-green tank top?

I don't know if my grandmothers ever talked to each other.

Do you know that idea about if you image something it will be true?

There are probably images in our lives which will never be actualized.

Particularly ones about the North.

Information is definitely not narrative (or maybe narrative isn't narrative).

Could someone (and I don't mean in the Japanese sense at all) clean out the culverts on the road in case there's a real deluge.

Sean's here too.

The food's mediocre.

I'm hoping to go to Regina for Saturday.

I've been fighting a cold.

Tomorrow I'm going to get a ride to town and then walk back. It's three miles.

I've discovered when I talk about a poem I'm too "academic." This worries me but maybe it's okay. Like, I don't think it's a serious problem. But if it becomes part of a life-force blowout I'll really wonder.

Don't forget to check the water in the batteries in this hot weather.

What does *Qu'Appelle* mean?

For all that place
hidden behind glass
and silent tortoiseshell stone
rocks for eyes

further
walked footsore for years
just to have a look
snuck up on smouldered night
seen cloaked by day

sudden silence stolen
into the middle of a conversation
the borderline
of a crowded room

by stealth
wealth taken

isn't there a kind of after-trauma
of the duplex mode
not quite sudden recognition
more like being struck dumb
loss of memory

just brushed
just passing through

The harbour's for the ear and the view. Out there a minor fourth foghorn claims large chunks of life. Sun glints off a powerboat windshield. Someone waves between waves, disappears. Boats bob. Risky staring

Victory Square
lots of chairs
for sitting on
outside in

Sillowing of work buzz at the edges, kitchen shadows. Sudden departure. Pecky meandering. Drumming day.

Hermes is a package of crackers

in Ierapatra
a motorbike
a taxi stand
a tour agency
rent-a-car

broken windmill spokes
solar water heater
man on a donkey

a blue plastic bag
a red plastic bag
a hotel in Rhodos

Turkish

Hermes is a snack bar
at the corner of Georgiou Kyrmixali
and Nikolaou Plastira
smoking

a hotel near the Plaka

and he comes from the mouth of an animal
on top of a cement mixer called Heracles

Are gods everywhere? There's a goose sitting on a nest on top of a piling. What at first I thought was her mate isn't. Turns out to be a loon, further out, bobs, then looks, pokes its bill into the lake, under. Looks down from that noonday above. Poke, poke. Beyond the birds the mountains. A trail turns around a large boulder. Subito.

Hrbr

water
scooters
boats fish

eat out
at night
and a light

house har-
bour kalimera
ave maria

hawa
evening
our mothers too

havoc

Men's mothers and the doorway bavardage. Arms folded, hips to post, toe tapping. This is the shore, the ebb in ebony.

Cretan wheels scribble
push at the walls of the island
night after long night

Translate coop and the desire for a perfect fit. Kaboom. Snap a vector until some word for steering gets there. Gyproc or wood.

"if one falls and ..."

jet-skyed
sand-filled
star-specked
girl-drenched
steel-netted
feet-pressed
house-whited
mortar-channelled
sun-paired
sandal-quiet
wrist-brushed
heart-weighted
"rock-hung
chain ...
broken"

Not this is what you see but this is what you say. You seeing. This trip a kind of samskara *to scare out the europe ghosts. It's as close as you've come to the old, old world – dead, dead europe. But you say it simplex, just to yourself. That's no good for these similes, one, then many. The world needs to be talked to, sung to. Some blind thing or poet. Some word rivering alongside.*

double bone and all around the fish images of northern lakes all of them or each one freezing over with latitude and the double bone comes out of the mouth with a warning to the tongue and throat then what about the fish scale skin and human face frozen thereafter or before in such a fish thinking ahead of the fisherman the catch and the slip of the tongue to make the hook hold curious places in taste here such ice water imaging cast up into the mouth I mean from the driftwood and all that grey and white breeding

SECOND PICKEREL

imagine the bird as a fish swimming those ducks
streaks eating weeds stuffed skin crisp bone dry also
sing about going straight ahead to China carp or ling
cod on the walls of the water and being there is all
it takes for the sky to feel full of Canada Geese over
any watery world now and osprey jet blue burst or
propel coloured name after some other lake you don't
know but with fish now think of those feathers wet
and smooth as contrail

THIRD PICKEREL

strange to think so much fish on the prairie subject of
Pleistocene history and sedimentary scalar too K. said
Winnipeg was a dish the city an old lake bed then
horizon seems more than flat so ocular to look up
out of this old water at sky and beach line precision
and quietness of the noonday pond solitary vector of
fish or insect surface actually bubble-tension again
that learning-to-swim horizontal ladder notion not
climbing to but through the stars

FOURTH PICKEREL

Homer you wanderer home again imprinted ocean
through implant by foreknowledge feeling the fluid
map to get to the fighting of the mind against being
taken spelled out clearly to itself the right idea of the
right ocean river or creek to the very gravel fighting
the mind against not getting there home again home
again to the heart that stellar steering of the passage
junction box genetic to contain the image you didn't
know any better it wasn't as if she might have been
waiting for you home is so singular nothing else is
appropriate to the mind which carries it so easily
hero this is it when you get there and back again
now we know that's why Helen said so

FIFTH PICKEREL

Gimli's pickerel cheeks for lunch the mountains
distant snow I thought Lake Winnipeg via Gimli
Peak in the Valhallas could be looked at there but
here soft tender pocket or flesh pouched as frozen
or upheaved waves of ice Pauline thought caught
in mid-air such leaps under the surface under the
belly got carried away to all those foreign european
countries even until being there later the snow corn
the high hot sun the cheeks flushed

SIXTH PICKEREL

walleye at the Bemidji Union voices in the train
broiled he says to do the cheeks in wine or beer
but the flounder w/ shrimp vision of the right
brain O Canada a pike they call it nothing to match
hemispheres in the drive for the perfect fresh sky
looking up out of Digby Gut's right finding bottom-
feeder flesh somewhere bluer and cold glacier line
projected into the ten thousand lakes across a water
border invisible except to unseen electromagnetic
rivers running through the starry way reflected in
the lake no wall was

THE WATER, THE FISH

twenty-third of January after the full-moon fish
frozen new-year cheeks all day salmon spawn
radio yak yak on the silted creeks
thawing Slocan River and Grohman's mouth iced all winter long
and there was Nancy from Nemo across the street
know my half-life this year turn around now to get home
with all of it, the map intact
imprint print

APRIL OR MAYBE MARCH

just this chance touching of you each night
this buildup in the bones under sleep's murky plans
this reservoir of unfamiliar language
near you this disturbed tug of body limb
heart-logged this shore or that
this flailing mind behind your tired sighs all that
core, root

all night the assizes of the years
holds this life at revised angles and intervals
his clamour for America's eyes
all around us "small month's meagerness"
every day precious tonguings accent a fever
words float through the dark freer than ever
do you know what I mean, this
feeding at the creek mouth
while we wait for the final coordinates

GETTING THE SIGNAL CROSSED

I'm thinking of Steve and how he'd say all these *things*.
The cool air laps at the open window. Cars drive around
up and down the streets, such beautiful bodies, he'd say.
The world of the soul is lost to the mind. St. Augustine.
It's all your fault. Smoke from the mill indistinct
from the mist grazes along the mountain shoulders (localized
showers in the trees). *Syntax* comes to town this week.
The images don't count, T.V. says. To be a woman,
think of a god. (Steve just smiles. He has eyes.) South America
comes a little closer. Tiahuanaco fingers the sky with thought.
Tacticless among the trees. Last night this was called
"Getting the Signal Crossed." Notes on history
to play with. Music – you don't know when it's going to stop.
Call it "Sammy the Salmon" and come home.

WHAT PREVAILS

the trees this morning and the clouds
today the same old mist-hackled mounts argue
the stability of the unchanging present
every day my mind drives up the road along the lakeshore
valleys of unavoidable distances on the shoulder
when what prevails isn't rhythm
but the poet's death
(they think)
on the eve of a new fascism
the kokanee have forgotten the way home
the spawning channels will be there long after
the rust Todorov says Poetry protects us from
even that line a trace of old track
whole geographies, continents, pass by
there's a light February snow today
and a loop in the sememe
that lets me dance.

THE STAIRS

to Bob and Smaro on the Star River

I always thought of stars on your stairs too.
Rising from that prairie "dish" up to thought, thinking
and the talk talking huge night sky
always something like the "emic" displacement
hovers in the rush of frozen air through the door
(how smart the builders are
to place it at the foot of the stairs
like a decompression chamber, up
and up literal to vertical possibility in your two minds
your voices unmeshed and scattered by desire.

I'll tell you, the stairs are perfect,
still used for each step of the return.

ACCIDENTS OF COLOUR 1

Everyone I know here
gets dressed up for winter
dreaming

so much brown, pink, so
much cold
Mary's scarf, little fur toque

red coat boat white
"writing my seeing"
riding my sea out

ACCIDENTS OF COLOUR 2

Colour my hat
McNaughton

the blue blue sky here on the prairie
you chose or was it
the yellow nearly mustard wool

stripes knit, horizon
plus the sun too and the frozen land
bright in a short day

such spaces, deserts, wasted words
I look at my watch and walk

you decide.

ACCIDENTS OF COLOUR 3

Pam's pretty red boots
orange beaded feet blue
mind signals thinking body connected
but strung to the storm outside
the letter *e* floats
(electronique)
in the dish, on the horizon
let through the snow
fed to the sign

albescent on the South Saskatchewan overbody

all air and larger, grasses and smaller

if you face north it changes

                                        cutbank

                                        into the mind

unexpected brown twists, nothing to stop the eye

therefore nothing there outside nothing

or just a little pink

                              (yesterday when it rained

everything

WINTER DAY

We expect more snow today and the birds will have to put up with it and so will all small things. Trees' limbs outlined by the snow they carry. All the dark things in winter. In the cow pasture behind our house the apple trees are frozen stiff and underneath the snow the first frost has been driven into the dirt. This large quietness, even with the train whistle in the valley, is the soft underbelly of snow clouds settled in the mountain trenches, caught in the trees, against the rock faces, electric lines hum the warmth between our minds and our homes.

ALPINE

the small grass
clings to the alpine scree
seed head heavy
breeze-frozen
rock

•

we want some of that autumn orange
that yellow, and that, and that
and give us more
of that dead red too

•

two days after we picked our dead mountain bouquet
I have thought three times at least of the wave sounds on some beach
and now the cello and shakuhachi
low roar of the wind up the slopes

•

the transparent and the brittle
this is all I do as I touch them
they break
bald anemone, dry
arnica seed
paper-clean

BLUE GROUSE BASIN

for Wendy Hurst

I knew when I came down the trail
and saw the shine in your eyes going up
all words for this day were yours.

frost-nipped huckleberries
sorrel maybe by the mine shaft
fennel (I believe the colour of maps
more than anything else)
snapshot of toe-baby and fireweed
alone now in this first snow meadow
water so pure, Plato
would have changed his mind

SPRING GEOGRAPHY

Things appear suddenly
not new but as they remain
left over from the winter

for example, dead logs
caught in the brush at all angles
a breathing pushes out of them

a picture in the warmer air
sings out
to the surfaces of our skin and eyes

a handful of dead fingernails
I love you today
like I have never before

fingers and hair, dead logs
heads hands twigs sticks
leaves grass the suddenness

and warm air shimmering
off the hood of a green
'47 Dodge pickup

mountains
come out of the clouds
the road down
to the lake

SORREL LEAVES

for Nancy Jean

got those sorrel leaves in mouth
taste of rock sand as root deep down
underneath as mineral water brought to leaf
large glass mirrors that cast argenta taste
remembering a place east of yourself
(old lakes)
the memory of view strata layer
to register glacial rivers milk as sorrel outwash
green leaf sediment eyes horizon mount
saint helen's hair and taste of years

WRITING THE TRANSLATING

for Jenefer

west arm boats all time drift move and say left-over
Jenefer you'd know this view maybe from your north or
what remains of a blond genetic flow your body getting
back up from the fall the ocean of embarrassment
remember floating up from the ice into the heat of July
now thawed to a greener place so that what remains
is more than this lake which is likewise fed by water
from somewhere else in turn no mistake just a further
shore of driftwood incomplete.

BUILDING POEM

Try to get to sleep
build headers and roof pitches
make up the construct
windows, doors
snow sliding off into the abyss
what more can we do inside
build otherwise, renovate
make things just right

as expected
fix everything that breaks
store the wood
the chainsaw the snow blower the tools
the tools all over the place
everything hidden and lost
never know
the woodpile falls far away into the falling snow
what matters when you and I build at night
as sleep takes on the actual plan

the mind's plain or landscape
go out and snap a line
is there enough room
twenty feet by the width
height plum
to the tops of the trees sky
where will the stove be
will the sun hit its south wall
where will the rain run to

so on down
sleep comes
into the dream of the building
instead of seducing you
eyes shut travelling
over angles snowloads footings and beams
to the bifrost

HER HOUSE

Her mind and life-
time, yearning

for her life's
mind on it, heart

dance, literally
with her mouth

shoulders too
today years ago

I married her.
Outside, the distant glaciers

crack and groan
with the same desire.

OPENING UP TO YOU

opening up to you,
                                        baby
I thought we'd dance across the floor
always try to keep available they say
those others
the ones with perfume in the Massachusetts air
behind them

I say let's go
and then I can't
but you, you're gone
on a sea of smell
puffed out in front of yourself
spinnaker
making for the new world

TRANSLATING TRANSLATING APOLLINAIRE

vis-à-vis bp

SOLEIL
        the sun rolls off my back

cou

coupé
        the snow falls into the world

cold

        put yr boots on an' yr toque
        wax wing's brittle

older
        into the world a little

leaf   from the sky

sky
        from the sky

ANTHROPOMORPHIA

stickle ceiling
rain (that's the forecast)
joy

how do I know this will work

can't stop it
to the world

the hildergast

pole

connected if you're a mouse
river if you're a fish

morphia
falling
to the east
in the west

death's stick the tool

same thing
the symmetry of accident spills again
hands reach out to help, there's a Shell station on the right
bulrushes line the ditches, fence posts line the land
the hydro lines
get nowhere
joy stops
a rainbow settles it for the sky

PICKET LINE

on the picket line
we could dance like a bird
old magpie, woodpecker
raven the thief
caw and peck
wiggle and get sassy
speak the spike
strut the truth

WORDS ARE REALLY GUT SMART

make it look the way you want
that's what images want for
at the end

music is like that too, you know
exactly when
what's next in song

then right in the ear
sounds get together in cognizance
how

can you do it,
the words don't come from other worlds
each breath a time sign

remembers itself this once
between all the other words

far away

FLOWERS THAT I DIDN'T KNOW

and rivers
    (the mountains, everything you can hold
    you sit in, not

this spectacle of the silent life
and the desire which goes on without you, words
flow too
    (the tree a part
    so simple it stands
    and blossoms and blossoms

you needed to know the events
like light and food
where to go next
and you didn't
    (I'm thinking a flower a river a flower
    new sights of the new to remind mind

this pensive, this light idea
with the body, this
life of its own
    (the narrative symbiosis, bark cork
    to beach
    wood
    sand
    Williams's "lips"

all this movement away from one another is unnecessary
blame it on the city

thinking thinking outside the landslide
lying of the tongue, outright
lies of the trees – a little
wind and light snow to tell the truth
at the foot of the glacier
the water will lap the shore.

THE BIRD PART OF IT

Oar sticks in the lake. Moon and stars colourless.
This bird will get to be a part of it, you between.

China makes noise. When my mother read Pearl Buck.
Let's see – Pearl, Yellow, and there's that other one.

Grain of the sun which is the key to your thighs.
Luce meles I mean. Skilled as a rower, a waver.

Not for sport. Sail, sunset, etcetera.
Oarswoman, Tisserande, and the crows.

Stars are like that. Shove it.
Stillness is everywhere tonight. Pierceless rocks.

We say admiringly how the loon oars the water.
Heaven is simple. A river. My horn of.

Stars are genetic. Salt.
After all, those wounds are for her. Thus music, too.

Stone-meal, sin, plenty of it. That's advertising.
My little woman of the night. In Japan, it's true.

Puts or pushes or sticks or shoves his always.
-euse, euse.

MAYBE MY GRANDMOTHERS WENT NORTH

after David McFadden

Here I am on the Prairies again listening to a voice
telling me I should be further north. But I'm not
ready. There's no one else with me. The grass has been eaten
by grasshoppers or is all dried up. Every person I have known
in this landscape has moved to another town, but none of them
has gone any further north.

Neither of my grandmothers
learned to drive. I don't know if they ever had mushrooms
to cook with. It was pretty dry here then too. They hardly ever
smiled but when they did they were indoors. Maybe
the earth heaved with ecstasy, maybe not.

THE POEM CALLED SYNTAX

We live on the edge of a lake called Echo.
I love this notion that noise makes itself,
so the lake holds all noise in its depths
and when the dog barks it gets it from the lake.

About nine thousand feet above these lakes (all lakes)
there is a geometry of sound, something like Plato's cave of noise.
It is from that construct the dog's bark takes shape,
a re-sounding of an earlier bark conditioned by the alpine.

History and physics. Acoustic paradigms in a bog of algae.
When I tell all my cousins and friends about this
they'll come to live on the shores of this lake and clean it up.
From the balconies of their summer homes they'll ask a lot of
questions.

two bears from nowhere, at least
the mind brought back

fog in the valley
life, the hands tell

horse made of trees
a labyrinth of space and time silent

the bears quiet now
maybe the horse whinnies

just for a moment you don't want to know
too much

the bottoms of the trees become huge roots
gnarled, really, into this moment past being

WEATHER

Where I live
when I wake up to the morning's dark pillow
I listen for the plow down on the road
to find out
if it snowed overnight
or not
to the soft
snow's
silence
distant plow's scraping
distance, distances
down
in the valley

A SNOW POEM FOR PAMELA

I saw your eyes in the lift line today
crisp, just below freezing, words
caught in the treetops
blue sky and the hoarfrost line lifting to an incoming fog
there's more
later you're a mother breastfeeding in the lodge
the hill very white
and your eyes looking through the winter air
all over me these words
with only your smile
eternal events

JAVANESE MUSIC TO THE END

call for Duncan in Damascus
sounds like bells are like bells
the lines to the street
leave his stairway to the eye
onlooker
around the world travel
sounds like size/picture
the news *ta'wil* method serious
music soft and thinks about it
other places sounds minds
you and Dan in the ancient city

MARCH MUSIC

Sounds roll beautifully from the piano. A precious accent lines the air on this mountainside. The contemporary earth comes again, again sings, self-seeking, circumstantial, but with a drum, a drum: full dominant seventh rolled out on the white snow still left in the cow pasture of a mirror, ayee, all the work of the skin, thaw coming up through the gravel road, truth rests, that's right, in memory, symmetric and outside the silent, not so simple as the dogs barking at the shadows along the treeline. Thursday, think of the thunder ahead.

ALMOST

for Erika

Almost don't dare look at the sky these nights for the largest moon of the year October tells and a full red sky in the West too down to the rivers below Mount Sentinel huffing it such seasons this valley from our walk along the back road up past McDougall's tonight and the dogs dogs more bite in the air than memory all of a sudden we come up our road under the cedar tree Erika I know that's yours and your mom's moon again how make it imagic words to tell you I love you and here, here's some of this hillside of your heart's such a large large sky.

BIRTHDAY POEM

for Erika

the dog said woof woof real low like he was talking to you
he said let's go I'll follow you or grohw grohw far back in
his throat watch out out there now the dog is a log on the
beach floating in our dreams he appears when you need to
cross water or brush your teeth in this world we take our
dog everywhere we go even over mountain passes in early
October just to remember each year lapping lapping the
same sure shore

PERMANENT SPIRIT

the "permanent spirit" turns
pages, the lexicon turns to
numbers, names, and the vague outlines of names

(bare birch of November) nothing
remains after the words
wet leaves

cold substrate of the precessions
motions of the stars
the tongue literally sings through those signs

(buzz)-frost without the body
unable to unscatter the scatter
tremendous volume of light

this is their white bark which coheres
to each phrase, the rest soil
mountain, root-rock

clean tatters shed the mouth
book of the forest uncut hillsides
self-interviewed gutter what fork, sweep

I get up in the morning
and the cloudy skies are in my legs.

The news at the door lies
under the guise of someone else's pulp mill.

In the shower I smell creosote,
my brain drinks up the pressure-treated ions.

You choreospect around the kitchen all egg,
you say my eyes have dreamed nothing.

Your eyes. Mine squint from the winter sun,
they read about the world, foothills in the distance.

They read languageless heads subtract
language. No more poems until.

Each day depletes a little more mith (*sic*).
mouth logged – logos scaled and decked.

Her tall body twirls, bone-rippled ankles lift.
We could count, we could dance that way.

outside up
the hill
Blackie's full
load of
hemlock spruce couple
sticks of cedar Meadow
Mountain to Lardeau six
teen minutes eleven
seconds re
carbo
nation

HOW TO GET ACROSS THE RIVER ANY RIVER

Drive northeast to a point on the old road
where you join a cortex of scars left by loggers.

After the container stop and look north
below the ridge the mouths of two small caves.

The veins are filled with words, stories really,
the further away they extend, the more striated.

Just our luck to live here on this side of the valley
on a hill with a perfect view

and a garden. Has the gutter on this
page, this old paper bridge, washed out

yet?

THIS IS ABOUT CHILE

The credit bureau phoned for his address today
but I told them I've lost touch.

Him asking me, then me talking you. Winnipeg and Nelson
diagrammatically arising from the dry horizon.

Why don't you right now try hard to be
about Chile?

Have a cup of coffee, sit in the morning air
look at what they do, pucker your eyes and ears.

Say *siempre*.
But it's only biology.

Come back to the numbers.
Pay your phone bill.

COW POEM

Sticky with frost
Sleeping with fire

I am a cow
Caught in a storm

My eyes open
Legs arthritic

Heartsore from dream
My mouth nailed shut

I can smell smoke
The snow is dry

On my shoulders
Gate of apples

Open ridgepole
Sky of grey words

Numbers as trees
Thick solitude

We don't get it
Such a long ride

Is this ocean
On the level

P. YOU SO

too fast fifty years you're still waiting to dance
antics of old migrations cut through your glance
I want to be with you under every tree
in the hills you hurtle smiles and tongues
scree vectors your legs, stride as you move
miles and miles the rice waits simmered
a little polka in your eyes this tilt of your shoulder
hands counter the air you ride so high o
five o five o content's continent so
wanna dance

FIVE ONES FOR P.

Watch you
and then keep
watching you.

More the body, everything
you've touched
tongue and shoulder,
shoulders
dancing too.

I keep watching
you out there, star
you sail, your sky, your moon
all night long almost
shore to shore.

When I'm out there with you
only to be with you,
why else
you're what I know, see you
always have to.

THE BEARS

All the trees around here are full of bears. Tonight
there is a full moon crying. Friends are upside down.
Animals are trying to think about life for a change.

In the hard light of the spruce trees dusk invites the geese.
Sometimes twice a year the cutthroat trout find the horizon,
the one that sits at the far end of the lake. Children.

Listen, to the cages being rattled. Look in their eyes
and look underneath the cedar boughs. All of us,
no matter how hard it is, plan trips to the prairie.

WHITE LAKE

The clouds
and the sun over the Pacific
mistakes about the atmosphere
and voices. And the "Gulf's" connection
with this woman's frame, Doña (?)
Malinche, Cortés's golden sun
except this is a Pacific cloud bank
(not interested in the thing itself) flying over White Lake
these hills, lines, and lakes the soft snow folds
even coyote in the valley forgets,
even the sparse pine on worn ridges, soft,
soft, even this sprinkle, this edge,
this cold and frozen grass
between our toes.

IN THE MAIL WITH YOUR LETTER IS A PACKAGE OF COUPONS

for Tom Wayman

minus thirty and they have to deliver this:
order this unbreakable coffee server now
never walk around again
a golden opportunity
forbidden fruit, to go
récoltez 18 cents de Croc-en-ble
solid brass
there is only one
personalized gift
made a little softer on your pocket
world's first $100
take strokes
keep your car or boat
free
scarios, the new lunchtime treat
your little monsters will gobble up
free career
how much do you know
introduce your family to our family
a personal message from Jean Philippe-LaFrance
économisez
wrap yourself in satin
30 cents de rabais
off
win a beautiful day
slice yourself in
get cracking
tastes fresher than fresh
try another variety
if you love
bet your kids ... and we're not bluffing
on light-flow days
send for the new

You want to know until I found you and your skin which sits in itself language was to me a system out there others thought up but I couldn't.

That story of the moon about her eye knocked out isn't what they told me.

You see. I don't remember any other than the sun-and-moon stuff or mountain mystery almost as "truculent and fingerless chamaco" better to be the bird or owl of poetry so I could just do it by itself without being surrounded by these masters of the "arrow" I don't know the surface of unless "it" literally is techne art is the only environment this paper and all the touch brought to that skin I know the action I'm capable of'll only get done by blood as the life of the mind thought not so silent just thinking of God rather the log sun scooped out his boat from or the cedar Enki drummed with I know exactly every time story happens I have memory back.

Breathin' My Name with a Sigh

(1981)

PREFACE

Deep Purple. 1939. This is a book of remembering. I am trying to clarify what the language carries for me, the ontogeny. Somehow a selection of the information of a life is made and placed in such a way as to not only make note of it but also to allow it to generate a truth otherwise impossible to locate. But the book is a "draft," since each incision (the beachwood, bookwood, and so runes, etc.) changes the whole thing it is a part of. To select out a pattern of things having to do with any of it has to do with all of it. One of my teachers told me "ontogeny recapitulates phylogeny" and that makes more sense to me now.

I want to thank Karl Siegler and bp Nichol for helping with some of the clarification.

Fred Wah
July 1981

I like the purity of all things seen
through the accumulation of thrust
forward especially the vehicle
container maybe/or "thing" called body
because time seems to be only *it* appears
to look into the green mountain valleys
or through them to the rivers & nutrient creeks
where was never the problem animal is
I still have a name "breathin' it
with a sigh"

Loki Death Dog Died

from out of his stomach
death   uyh   uyh
cousin snow mountain
died
his death
along his right side he lay
uyh   uyh
with his mouth
and his hunger/love
with his twisted stomach
he runs (I run)
along the road
to the trees/sky
uyh   uyh   uyh
such a hard breath
from the pit of the stomach
hard
death
scattered
clouds in the sky

stomach

inging
day song
instrument

aying it
each time
throat

ing lip
lip

eyeing
for sure

bells
long, long days
in the mountains

ringing it
wire

ight
all day
sun

ing
near foreign
music
mming it
to myself

What else was there outside in the dark but night
which has always been and is an answer
trick presence to the daylight you've seen
every day you'd think, eh?, and not
simply everything over and over again forever and ever, right?

Are origins magnetic lines across an ocean
migrations of genetic spume or holes, dark
mysteries within which I carry further into the world
through blond and blue-eyed progeny father's fathers
clan name Wah from Canton east across the bridges
still or could it all be lateral craving hinted
in the bioplasmic cloud of simple other organism
as close as out under the apple tree?

Words fly from our mouths as leaves
fall to the ground from the trees in fall
"We eat. Everything
stares back at us.
All this hunger is what we call the World."

Wind and rain
(no pain

just a storm at the cave mouth howling
leaves rasping the pavement
and water
a river of it also
falls to the mouth

(the Yangtze, the Columbia

Ocean

Ocean Ocean

lick

the shore.

(the Shore?)

Father, when you died you left me
with my own death. Until then I thought
nothing of it. Now I see it's clear-cut
both genetic "bag" as well as choice. I know now
I'd better find that double edge between you
and your father so that the synchronous axe
keeps splitting whatever this is the weight of
I'm left holding.

I thought where I came from we grow up also
only to reach heaven
and/or what our bodies dictate to us.

Sometimes I remember the "hinge" too late
or the "fence"
having crossed from side to side.

Such "things" and their ideas demand me
return just as the dogs outside in the winter
scratch at the door to get into the warm house.

I wonder if I can ever pay attention like that
to my own life and the simple or bare particulars
of what is its "number" without making up
some other cruel paradigm to swim around in.

It's April and I feel the water running
but I don't know how to count on it
                                                    or where.

mmmmmm

hm

mmmmmm

hm

yuhh   Yeh   Yeh

thuh moon

huh^{h} wu   wu

unh   unh   nguh

w________h

w________h

Now know why you missed dreaming
for so long how could you sleep
in the darkness without a sphere. I think
I'd better get back there pretty soon myself
or shift off that surface each of us lives upon
for ourselves day to day. Can't get it
or at least it's hard to hold on
until I think of her return, look
up behind our place into the field
full of cows and apple trees take the whole
thing and run outside with it from the night
into the day with a promise
of at least an echo.

Not so much all of us dying
or nobody else living or even one
one shining master of light
but a procession forth
into I like the movement
in our syntax goes
something like a river Daphne
so it's still "how" we do what
and give a punch we hope words
to take off on us dying to do that
the best way we can

If I don't pass the impasse what'll happen?

Maybe I can stay

                    right where I am

until thinking about it

settles like dust through the sunshine

and gives it all back to me

so I could just pack up each day like that maybe

no one does anyway

at least look like they do

do what they're doing.

I lie here and wait for life again
no one told me this happens
not death but a consequence of it
the physical isn't a world
at least it wasn't this morning
when I ran up the road out of breath
yet that is what I most desire.
Information. What leads up to death,
is only information.

It's not enough. I think it should be.
To be able to. That's all I need.
To do anything. Complete.
How does it go? Did it?
I want to know. I'd better.
What's going on. Or *it*.
I shovelled gravel today. I hoped
that would be enough but then afraid
of a trace of myself   left
somewhere else   far away in the mountains alone
I thought working hard in the hot sun
I know how that goes. I would just breathe
but away from me. Out. Give it all
back.

the buildup
how I listen to myself make it
"hold on"
so that the day remains open
the next collision in the light
and catch up to the breath
breathing somewhere
the air

as it comes out ahead of me
wah^{h}, wah^{h}

No foolin' I thought I was gonna die
just about every day so much the mountains
air clear blue sky & hum broke up
as pieces each of themselves I was separate from
larger than life the thought my face hands all
action bigger my picture of head arms fingers sens-
ation at first something from mother my eyes
at sleep birth
swelld up like the stung finger head information
creek the first time in McNaughton's
January 1974 to know it's true even
the enlargement now remember
more?

Brother then brothers
number/age
"a matter
of penetration"

the three of us
someday take that on
each one of us
older then
than father

brothers

lines co lure added up into placed
numbers games matrices objects such as trees
designs parents children thinking
all about it all the time you believe
it's mother but you you're the one
indexed here too thought up by living
at once feeling the ten commandments
part of the mountain or father caught
into the typology stuck with the gender
listed calendar birthday interstitched
I thought world and the beauty of language
as a system too to reinforce the continual
buildup and impression on the life of itself
so at any point it knows there are those three
as well as itself plus objects as voices
texture too fits in the right spot

Bank the fire
embers and wood
my life not away from itself out there
not breathing
watching it die
watching it
saying it

firelight breathing eyes orange

set the draft

wuh^{h}

cut sweat and cord the wood outside in the cold snow for the winter
split and the night falling in the winter in the winter
mouth says it
vapours
to cool the soul
no, to cool the heart
he says (Aristotle)
on breathing
animal

the first bridge was in Trail
and it crossed over the first river
full of fish and it moved with weight
not speed the first mountain
a hill of sand and scrub brush
Ernie's dog Mickey died
it's where Donnie was born
the Trail Smoke Eaters
were the World Champions

A form
container

my mind
dialogue

logos
words, everything

but pictures
stitches

wounded
knees.

this gash
this one about breath
up a mountain for example
I have this warning, six toes
and a mouth three arms
and a head with hair
called proportional thought
I wait for the dance to start
but know it will
end up sliced across
the size of my head
hands much larger up there
mind doesn't tell me
until now it starts "time"
and again own up to it
image-works
falling up through the sky
like houses

outside it's snowing

they're skinning the bear

snowing

a small she black bear

symmetrical paws

knife

slit

down the inside thigh

to the crotch

careening

single sound flies from her

from her

the snow falls

from her

flying from her

naked now

bear pig hamstrung, flesh

a little fat (winter)

from her

death   stick's   tool

each of us the implement

extension arms legs mind

think it out by counting fingers

not killing but planning I've meant to do that

all my life

Flesh, as if
to eat it up

fresh surface
hair on my arm

a chunk from your cheek
teeth

your song
shattered on its own words

words in mouth
chewing, chewing

words which mean
is are here

taste, broken
bones

dead fingernails
hair, voices

he wiped his mouth
on his sleeve.

mother
somewhere
remember
whoever
forever
to fly over
love her
pleases her
caress
close
careless
loss
most
moist
remove her
mutter
mummy
maybe
habit
added up
puddled
mud
cleaver
pie
calamity
dust
wax
because of her
house
window
Saskatchewan
radio
air
breath
quiet
just
Mary
baby
lady

cream
Swede
more-to-me
names
remember her
corrine
kar en
clean
heart
core
remember you flying over me mommy
outside a moist loss
touch & float

okay I get a sense of it now
breath can reach my toes
take there the thought
and the breath goes with it
simple exercise mechanics
image disconnected out
beyond the foot
remember *hw* *hw*
question and answer remember
the only bird of poetry
untitled, "buried at Smoky Creek"
at night
Sanskrit "to breathe"
out only empties the container
a handful of dead toenails
hw *hw*

sounds of o and ree
tryi-, try to make breath
sounds that make (sky)
mine (me) to breathe
                                        (see breath
                                                out in front of myself
                                                as a white mist in the winter air

or some schoolteacher read us a story
about the Arctic and how cold cold is
so cold someone's words had been frozen in the air
and years later when it warmed up
language popped out right in front of them
right out of the air
breath
which makes sound from my body
air which flies out of me
through o and ree
ooooory   ooooory

breaking open as spittle would crackle in the frozen air

                                      crystal

as he leaves her
as he moves from her
for the whale hunt
as he leaves
he blows his breath
into a kelp bubble
shaped like a small balloon
ties it off and gives it to her
to keep for him
his air
until he returns
or so she'll know he won't
when it deflates
                    around her neck
she wears his breath
or over her bedpost at night
his breath

(horizon of ocean swell and tide
something like old sealskin
strip of seaweed necklace
box of cedar
air
you hold for me
till I get back)

The River
is the Milky Way
the map
of the River of Heaven
shows where Tisserande
and her former husband
the herdsman
separated by the river
once a year some ravens
carry weaver woman
across the river on their backs
to spend the night with him
hence "the horn of plenty"
or egret feathers
and this alone of all the universe
endures but a single day
the fete of womanhood
family, conjugal bliss
this is the seventh month
Virgo, and there is a dipper
seen coming down through the night sky
to all of us.

Tisserande
I you and me
even the crows
all the children still to come
see this story in three stars
and watch our selves
coincide
for a River.

so what's left over
        ruins
                hard granite along the sides of the roads shine
in the moonlight above the river the highway follows to town
so whatever
                snow
seasons of
                        I'll tell ya what
ruined
she said
        stoop
                                cut "breath"
heaves like that through her body at the worst of times
comes over her like you wouldn't believe jarring her head
you might say
                so
people do
                when we can or have to
                                                God's candour
something, something or other
highway travels
through the wood
all kinds
        keeps us warm gets us there to the towns
houses lights late afternoon they're plowing the road
as the snow falls a bit more each day everybody going
don't keep what is left over
I need it.

I like the simple truth in Lawrence's ", really"
at the end of his line
being alive he calls it.

The sounds of a river

ree   ree   ree

and part of the colour of that water and the night
blue and slate vision over river in the sky
runs through all the stars last night morning
out over the lake light (picture too) into dawn
horizon mountains.

Never wonder much which one is that
or that star in mind's eye but this looking at them
this ride on out.

Cups in the rocks along the shore
rock water gatherers sandpipers skirt their beach

reh   ter   ter

and a lot of words like soul air breath saiwala
day work eons message death map count on it forever
head underwater water sounds gurgle over creek stones
granite

or eyes in sky sound the same
birds' chirps fill up the world left over from the night
heads full and black till daybreak breaks
beaks get through bumps in the night sky
to daytime close to sounds and colours effervescent.

Breathe dust like you breathe wind so strong in your face little grains of dirt which pock around the cheeks peddling against a dust storm coming down a street to the edge of town in Swift Current Saskatchewan or the air walked out into the fields across from Granny Erickson's house with a few pails of water to catch gophers over by the glue factory downwind of all the horses corralled their shit and hay smell whipped over the grass and the smell of prairie water as unmoved water doesn't move is stale or even rancid but the air along the prairie road by Uncle Corny's farm first thing on a clear summer Sunday morning and in winter how the snow smelled like coal when I maybe later in Trail B.C. up the alley behind our place my mother needed water to melt on top of the wood cookstove so she sent me out with my sleigh and a galvanized washtub to collect the snow so dirty in the city I scraped off the top few inches before I put my shovel in and then packed it into the tub and back to the house and stove air hot and steamy pink over the stove my mother what did she need that water for I don't know but where somewhere the snow smelled like coal or is it back in Swift Current the cold so cold it smelled of cold I don't remember maybe we had oil there we did later in Nelson and I had to go out into the shed and pump a bucket of oil from a forty-five-gallon drum for the stove in the living room but the shed had a coal bin too coal for the stove in the kitchen at night coal dust even later filling up Pearson's furnace hopper every three days move it shovel full across the basement the dust even later in the summer play anywhere someone's coal bin settled into my nose and the oiliness of it on the skin I rode down the hill outside the house on Victoria on a coal shovel I hit a rock and had the wind knocked out of me I was dying and couldn't even tell anyone as they walked by but stood and waved my arms and flailed the message without air

my father hurt-
ing at the table
sitting hurting
at suppertime
deep inside very
far down inside
because I can't stand the ginger
in the beef and greens
he cooked for us tonight
and years later tonight
that look on his face
appears now on mine
my children
my food
their food
my father
their father
me mine
the father
very far
very very far
inside

Poem lightens the lungs Diana says meaning
birds which fly away into the air disappear
words end up relief of carrier message also take
away the little smoke a residue the dual nature
which flight up & out is part too so tight heart so core
all such acts breathe vocals and sigh (say).

have to do
he has to do things
today one
after another
many things
think about
(he's looking at himself)
doing
he has to
have to
what does he have to do today
to do it before he does it
seeing it
then he looks out the window
through the trees and up the hill
just he, it, that, there
out there everything
have to do with it

WHAT'S IT LIKE TO HOLD YOURSELF IN
SETTLE FOR THAT
A WHOLE LIFETIME
NO TIME NO CONNECTIONS (CONNECTIONS)
HOME UP THE HILL AFTER WORK LUNCH BUCKET
EVERY DAY ANOTHER DAY
EYES GLAZED UNDER THESE MOUNTAINS
SKIN TIGHT
NEVER WENT
PLACE NOPLACE

TO HANG ON TO
KEEP UNDER YOUR HAT
(THE RAILROAD HAT)
LOOK LIKE YOU DO
DO WHAT YOU'RE DOING
FISH IN THE RIVER ON SUNDAY
LIVE NEXT DOOR
FIX THE FENCE
INSIDE

THE HOUSE YOU ARE SO YOUNG
OLD DOESN'T
YOUR DAUGHTERS DO, THEY GROW UP
AND THERE YOU KEEP STANDING WALKING
CHISELLED INTO THE SIDEWALK
THE TOWN THE MOUNTAINS ON YOUR BACK
RIGHT TO YOUR GATE
TO HOLD YOURSELF IN
NO SNAP
NO OTHER MEN
THEY GO AWAY DIE
THEY'VE ALL DISAPPEARED
BEFORE YOU OUT OF YOUR WAY, ALL
OUT OF YOUR WAY

WANT RIVER PIECE OUT OF THIS MOVING RIVER ████ TREES BANK
FLOWS ALONGSIDE █ PASSES BY FLATHEAD THINK ABOUT IT FAR
AWAY IN THE TAMARACK STANDS ██████ NIGHT BURNING
IN THE RIVER ██ IS A HEAVE, A HEAVEN ███ ALONG THE █
HORIZON LANGUAGE COMES ██████████████████████████
THAT WAY TOO ALONG A RIVERBANK HERE SEE IT RIVER WATER
███ COLD ██ GREEN MURK GREEN RIVER GREEN GREEN ██████
SMOKY GREEN ██████ MUD GREEN COLUMBIA GREEN GREY FLATS
███ VISTA VALLEY LARGE ███ ON A SMOKY DAY SKY BIGGER
LAKE ██ START THE KOOTENAY ██ WHAT CAN YOU SAY █████
A RIVER TALK ███ TALK TO IT ███ RIVER ██ MOVE DIFFERENT
████ BODY ████ MIND ████████████████████ ALONE ALSO
████WITHIN THE BANKS IT ITSELF TRAVELS FRAME SHAPE █████
TERRAIN CLAY BANK LANDSCAPE ROCK WALL AND BEACH ██ WATER
HEAVIER ███████████████████████████ ON THE EARTH'S FOLDS
UNDER COYOTE UNDER EARTH ████ WHERE ███ MOVE ITSELF DOWN
INTO THE EARTH GROUND ITSELF BY ITSELF IN ITSELF HOLDING
██████ CONTOURS RIVER HOW DO I TALK TO YOU WHEN YOU
███ SOFT SOUNDS USUALLY QUIET NO SOUND RIVER INTO LAKE
██████ RIVERS ███ SWIFT ██████ SSSSSSSSS ████████ SHHHHHH
OOOOOOO KINDA GROANING █ AS IT MOVES ITSELF ALONG THE ELEVATION
█████ GROANS UNDER THE WEIGHT ████████ MAYBE THE WEIGHT IS
EARTH GROANING █████ SOMEBODY ████ GROANS ████████████
KEEP INTO CLEFT ███ GET OUT OF █████ RIVER INTO LAKE
NO DIFFERENCE AT ALL ALL FLOWS LAKES JUST WIDER AND SITTING
THAN RIVER OK DIFFERENT COLOUR GREEN TOO ████████████ WITH
MORE WHITE FROM WIND CHIPPING IT UP INTO THE AIR HEAVES THE
LAKE INTO THE PHRASE ████ THE PHRASE ███ OF THE LAKE ██████ THE
PHRASE OF THE LAKE IS THE WIDE WIND SHIFT FROM NORTH FROM SOUTH
OK WIND TALKS THE LAKE OSPREY FLIES OVER IT ROCKS AND CREEKS
ALONG ITS BANKS THE BEACHES TREES JUST WIDER THE HEAVE MORE
SET RIVER ████████ INTO LARDEAU DUNCAN FEEDING/FEEDS ITSELF
INTO ITSELF ITS OWN WORDS WHAT WORDS DO A RIVER SPEAK HOW
WORDS COME WHEN YOU TALK TO YOURSELF YOU A RIVER ME A RIVER
HER A RIVER MOVING BODY HER/MINE RIVER MOVING BODY MOANS LIKE
████ THE RIVERS' WORDS DON'T COME TO THE RIVER BACK TO ITSELF
AS IF THEY WERE WATER ████████ YES THEY DO THIS THESE WORDS
COME OUT OF THIS RIVER THEY ARE HERE RIGHT NOW BECAUSE OF THE
RIVER AND I TRY NO THE RIVER DOES IT TRY ██ SO ██ THE WORDS
JUST AS THE RIVER THERE TO BE SEEN OR HEARD OR TESTED TAKEN
INTO THE VIEW WORLD BODY SIZE CLEFT GROANING COLOUR GREEN
PLACE BANKS CLAY GRAVEL BRIDGES ██████ TAKE US █████ TRENCH

IN THE ARMS OF THE FAMILY

IN THE ARMS

IN THE ARMS OF THE CENTRE

IN THE ARMS

IN THE ARMS

IN THE ARMS OF THE MIDDLE

THE FAMILY

IN THE ARMS OF MY FATHER

SKY

IN THE ARMS

MOTHER NIGHT

IN THE ARMS OF US ALL

OF US OUR HOLDING

IN THE ARMS

SHE WALKS / HE HOLDS

MY FAMILY

IN THE ARMS

WE ARE TOGETHER FROM

IN HIS/HER ARMS

HIS MOTHER'S MY GRAND

FATHER'S

ARMS

now you're not thirteen
now breathing
is easier
what's left
feels firm
going somewhere
your weight on your earth
feet and hands body
eyes and a mouth
something to say
to do with all of us
you're not sure anymore
but live in *your* world
every day
now
for nothing but the life
let's start
to look around again
but this time
let it go
    it go
    it go

all over

oh river

laba laba

rover more

move before

reema reema

come here

I mean it

lever lever

for ever

sever sever

wean lips

deer wan

wah water

wah water

when I will be water

was suh

in the distance

distance

ihh-zuh ihh-zuh

water

did you hear me

wa ter

wa ter

otter

[ah^{h}]

Loki is buried at Smoky Creek

He pointed at the water
he looked that way
towards the creek
then went there
through the fields to the west at night

aligned body fallen

flowed down mouth

the way the creek does

did

for Leni Hoover

Loki warned me
when I went to him
our body

muscle dog eyes
and stomach horizontal

death shoots straight through
feel it

your name is my name
our name is bones
bones alone names
left over slowly
to send signs forward
found out needed
knowing names
parts family imprint
left shape all over
us within it
name signed
me name
as our name
added-up knowns
become truths
said-again things
left over after
sedimentary hard
embedded rock to tell

Fish under yourself (self)
Spread out a bit (bit)
flap your arms (wings)

just counted for his death I
cried once privately and once
public – seven years later

the father entwined
those bones (two branches
or a towel twisted
to wring the water)

thought out empty
until I could count
on it. Him
and then me.

try it adds up to a colour
twice working over it
in the summer down to baseball

the kids play their music
P. draws a bath
(margins, numbers, and thinking about *it*
underneath

uh/schwa
arrows

three things
white in the next room
a number *L*
(a French sentence saying this)
the finest lyric cadence
voice near the sink
at the end of the day
gotta even it up
stomach knows
all the maps

"got" his eyes, sister
after the brothers
genetic it
you are left
with your own fatherness
the way you taunt
the men in your life
with his dark
dark brown eyes

breathing in the water so much a breath
to make a time times so simple rhythm
early snow mountain peaks body hair finger
nails the death past 54 measure know
nothing rotten smell histories it like
layers of froth the scarlet letters parts
of our genitals my breathing in the pool
lengths stretched father's parts out

Sigh.   a relief of muscles and blood flowing
from the deep with the little breath from the animal
walls of the cage within the body marrow
a shape to carry the trembling drum the
mad shoots of pure voice pure containerness
nothing but sighing says it

The diaphragm of the clouds above the ceiling of the sky the moon makes. The night. Sweep sleep. Dreams. I don't know that any of that matters because it was/is inconsequential (out of time) as far as the colour (white) remains glacial in the mind. There, is a place. The voice soon takes over. Try and try, it makes story out of the memory of an image, a time, colour. The formula for the moment is "digging." Therefore see if the language used in the story tells, reveals, itself, a self, a plan. If you go seven miles up Goose Creek you'll come to Raspberry Village.

Sigh. A tenuous slight stream of air escapes through a high point midway up the chest. At night, during sleep, this light puff of breath is part of running and falling.

Night and breath, the moonlight, him breathing hard as he walks along the black road on a cold November night, the stars wear thin. At least he's thinking that and then he says to himself "the trees" and "they are there as they have always been in the dream or in the memory of them." So the cold air condenses on his mustache and he blows out a puff of air which then glistens out in the moonlight as jewels in front of himself.

Home before you know it. The stove still warm. He talks to himself because thinking has become words in his mouth and the pictures from the day coalesce with the pictures of the night so that he talks in his sleep (he thinks). The language comes into the room with him and touches the sides of the stove, turns out the dining-room light, undresses.

Then the thin stream of air from his nostrils heads for his toes but before it gets there, before it settles into his bones, before it spreads out into the night, it sets out over a world.

When he wanted to stay alive but was drowning the sunlight soundless shafts of thin light just past his eyes and far away shouts beyond the film of water above his head water started to come into his mouth at the corners of his closed lips. When the strength of the river's rush pulled him under with hands grabbed out at but not reaching the pebbled rock surface his face broke the water with a cry and grabbed all the air it could and yelled that fish sound one world to the other.

to travel south
the thins
white
the cedar so heavy
forests
the ridges
snow
these things these
aloof
those tastes of
this taste
nada
mexico something else
death and wood
colour and death
a piñata
wisps of vapour
scents of track
touches
those larges
pieces
a calendar
with everything
made up

rivers breathe water
and that breath is a river
of itself the air, the water
the body the place
the flow forward
into thinking about it
flowing
in half
(halves)
one could drown in them
in myself
and that air swims out of me
a river lets go
in a body (ya hahhh)
figure it out wet
a river a breath
original a earth
(ahhh)

Father it is fall
the leaves turn
the hills
wait for winter again
the river and the town
the cars
reflect the sunlight
movement is in holding
bodies with the years
I am over forty now
they took down the Diamond Grill sign
Mother has returned from China

time
is an interference
with work
                    music
has shape   (splitting birch this weekend)

Father
again it is another season
the turning of it all
the spin
is sound
yet soundless at the core
to say this to you is nothing now
nothing
yet

the gap

breath comes to mind
vocalization
from the picture an ocean, you say
trees, trees a sky and the water
(water)

horizon side to side
colour already knows behind it
pushes out

my breathing as I look at your picture of a line which gives way at the centre and falls into the valley breathless then below the surface you've worked on I hold the cool silence and fullness there especially the emptiness the motion of falling into the middle outside it is the gully that runs from the orchard down past the house in your picture my breath then mind finds solace

for Leni Hoover

for
I forgot
memory
remembered
signs/words
a genetics
carries the deer
dance carries
the tree
& other forms around
something else thinks too
from somewhere in my body
carrying
the other for
ever
and ever.

So tight the trees didn't move
another ring of the soul said "breathe"
from the past presents itself forward
into the ring with a face of branches
antlers thought themselves on the head
everywhere around the ring of the moon
in the autumn sky trees danced with
deleaved outstretched the burden of
thought thinking about it as if memory
carries such intricacies of the world
time growth out into all of it from
inside.

to get it how the river in its mud flows downstream
how it goes mouth or breath fluid down to the toes
outside in the wind the dark and stormy brother's
sister's blood keep coming back into the word
alongside itself a bear and a bad man/woman family
blood keeps it now my daughters for the moon and
men and their own river a cleft in the earth going
colour languaging a feeling inside the surface feeling
out the breadth of my mother/father things I am also
left over thing put together calendar's event world
the children's things and wind last night/biography

the father grandfather
lineal
Grampa's smile
your walk his
smile

the grampa
eyes
your serious

my shoulders
his watch
your ring
him
thinking me
ahead of him/myself
"eight spot"
all of it
thinking
a chance

lineal
face, body
a hemi-
sphere

baseball (the)
westness, always
comes back
home, hit it
alike with yourself
your body (east)
compelled to return
the ball
hit by the boy
ten
and his brothers
soft oiled pocket
out
two diamond lines
ever widening vector
of chance ready
to get home
and shout into the air
and sky up
to twenty, times
multiplied
numbers the slowness
of spatial (person)
part of the body
travels
with the ball in mind

runs the cycle
the ground
under his feet
his breath in front of his face
words come out of
sun in the sky (trees, legs, eyes)
head says
it looks at itself
a quick truth
breathes
bleaches
his hair (cycle)
imagine saying it
say it "ground
    goes
    hold
    does"

a french word
travels through itself
to english
feet
truth
mouth

FORTY-FIRST THE YEAR THE STREET THE AVENUE
FORTY-FIRST AND THIRTY-SEVENTH AND ARBUTUS
A YEAR TIMES AWAY YEARS ADDED UP FORTY-
FIRST YEAR SPRING BEING IN THE SEASON NOT
SEEING IT AS DEATH DENIAL BUT THE WARMTH
OFF THE HOOD OF BLUE THIRTY-SEVEN DODGE
COUPE THE SAND DRIES BY THE TIRES IN THE
TREES ON VICTORIA STREET THE KIDS THEY PLAY
KICK THE CAN FORTY-ONE FIRST AND THE PLACE
CITY CAR BOY MAN SEES DEATH STILL THROUGH
EYES EASTER LILY SCARLET LETTER NEW YORK
EAST EDEN TIMES PLACE THE SAME SEEN EVERY
YEAR SIMPLE UNEVEN LOOKING FOR A CHOICE
A THING SIGNED AS THE PLACE TIME LATE ONE
NIGHT THE AIR IS SUDDENLY FILLED FOR MONTHS
AHEAD MARINE DRIVE AHEAD OF A BLUE SKY
SPRING AND ALL LOOKS BACK HIS KORA HEART
HE IN IT ALL THE TIME BLOWS WARM AIR INTO
HIS EYES FACE AND BACK LEGS ASTRIDE THE
LIFE FINALLY PLANTS TOMATOES AND PEPPERS
IN JANUARY FORTY-ONE TIMES FOR SUMMER TO
OPEN HIS MOUTH AND EAT IT ALL SPRING AND
GRANVILLE HONED INTO HIS PLACE ANY PLACE
BECAUSE IT'S THERE WHEN HE IS LITTLE BOY
IN KNICKERS WEARS SHORT PANTS AND GOES
FOREVER IN HIS LIFE LIKE THAT FOREVER IN HIS
LIFE HEART CORE CENTRAL DENIAL OF NOTHING
TAKE IT SPRING FORTY-FIRST MOUNTAINS STREET
PURE AIR LEAP INTO SPRING AGAIN.

World
house open to the music
scalar
          two hands
people, called "bavardage"
talk, a world
times time, we eat
the truth, food
(a piano) tune
her fingers
small talk, chatter
she breathes into her flute
this house and a music in each room
bodies hands legs lips mouthing
all the world
to say something talk
to eat (a foreign word)
connect, edit, sound, and get
to it

Once
made it
up.
Once
lied
about it.
Through
his teeth
passes
everything
he talks about.

A hight
e at beneath
the heaven
she heavy
over ethe
every as in
ide David

when you die it snows
late September mountain peaks

every time it happens, I see it
and I think of you then

your sister Ethel
she says white is unlucky

it snowed today at timberline
it's never very far away is it

each year at first snow
your death makes more sense to me

Breathless
news
full of information
inspired birdsong
within small body
carried airless
without experience
exed empty
caught (warbled)
in the throat

swimming for dying
underwater air easy
deep lung into stomach
sounds breathing bi-
labial muffled talking
to myself dreaming
for living
so far mouth
mouthing

trumpet
grammar
subject
subject act
predicate valve silver
tone gliss
water music
phrase, phraseology
study and concatenate
the sun set in the west
from here sounds make
I go on still "noisy"
lips diaphragm the air
meditate a line begins
and goes to pulls
deep liquid wire
to the bell, day
daying

waiting for Saskatchewan
and the origins grandparents countries places converged
europe asia railroads carpenters nailed grain elevators
Swift Current my grandmother in her house he built on the street
and him his cafes namely the Elite on Centre
looked straight ahead Saskatchewan points to it
Erickson Wah Trimble houses train station tracks
arrowed into downtown fine clay dirt prairie wind waiting
for Saskatchewan to appear for me again over the edge
horses led to the huge sky the weight and colour of it
over the mountains as if the mass owed me such appearance
against the hard edge of it sits on my forehead
as the most political place I know these places these strips
laid beyond horizon for eyesight the city so I won't have to go
near it as origin town flatness appears later in my stomach why
why on earth would they land in such a place mass of Pleistocene
sediment plate wedge arrow sky beak horizon still waiting for that
I want it back, wait in this drunken Christmas night
for that largeness of itself my body to get complete
it still owes me, it does

One more thing
a colour

pudeur

comes from voice mouth tongue creek
sign not tight a little red too chinese blush
but clear and right / clear and light
especially face, water, creek, tongue, mouth, voice
noise
voice skin
surface
shine flush
voice face
mouth shine
skin voice
face face
skin shine
blush water
creek tongue
colour flush
voice

ə

I
jazz

I sing
I do
just what
feels good

I play
the notes
of *it*
I swing
and talk back
sound that's right

I take the breath
through throat
and hold it
in the stomach
hit the fingers
on the horn

blow the jazz
that's where it goes

next spring

I'll go out to the garden

and with a stick

plant myself

and eat me in the fall

Grasp the Sparrow's Tail

(1982)

You never did the "horse" like I do now but walked
straight down the aisle of the Diamond Grill
and kicked the kitchen door with such a slap
all the way up to the soda fountain
I know it's you.

You played "timber" with your eyes and voice
and laughed always as you fisted the coins
deep secret gabardine pocket jingle and sudden thrust
hard out on the Arborite counter no chance
they try to get past your bluff.

You moved your body on the go even when you stood
head and shoulders arms too swing with the talk
rhythm to hard-working feet (I loved to shine
your alligator shoes, special, for going out only)
and then you died dancing.

July 28
In Vancouver just before trip to China and talk with G. of different ways the writing could get done. J.'s birthday.

Her a daughter's birthday think China book out linked to poetry each day something new apparent each word capable of total Chinese character baggage really gain sight of word's imprint to pose itself as action on the world in the context of the journey somewhere get ready for the Canton poem

Aug 1
Over the Pacific between Honolulu and Japan. Dreamt last night about a poem of me sitting on a bus-stop bench in L.A. but of course I couldn't remember it this morning, the poem that is. Just now while napping on the plane I dreamt of the words I missed but even now I can't remember them.

Thought of making part of book "the" Family can be known by initial as in J. and E. and Lh. but anyone else by full name could mean group caste imprint exotic typology genetic histories name language carries also later I get a small bloodstone chop with schwa for my sign others choose personal designs varietal identity, definition, red ink, lucky green, 8 spot, either on the body or not

The notes to what I could do rather than doing are always like that, thinking it out ahead of time. Obviously I'm in my mind too much and that enters dreamland too. But, I say to myself, keep the ears open for possibilities and leads. The two oriental languages on the plane are Korean and Japanese.

Japanese female language so light nearly a giggle or think of R. and his defiance the other night before we left now grammar how to question verb over noun equals situation picture how to staccato Japanese and something on colour or *pudeur* in dream too or just before or after

Aug 2

Wake up in Kimi Ryokan after arriving during typhoon in Tokyo last night. Had difficulty finding this place M. had told us about but from Ikebukuro Station we had the help of a Japanese college student. Walked through the pachinko neon and narrow back streets eyes wide, in the rain and sweating with the heavy bags. This syntax, have to reverse the English to fit, like

Tokyo
windy is
wind out in the ryokan courtyard
all night noise in the trees is

and think of different voices but I'm sore and tired this morning from that adventure last night

The others' voices in their poems sharp, his and hers, P.W.'s
clean bp's narrative thought then in the calm of the writing
in the morning also the Tosa Diary and my own journey
the danger of focusing on the particular, e.g., of the very
narrow stairs at Kimi stones set into the large hardwood
floorboards shine like tile the blueprint and architecture of
our six-mat room here

Aug 3

Dreaming in Tokyo. The margins of the page, the limits the "boundary walker" and Duncan's Shinto gate, the arche, the architecture, the roof beam (?), prime, oriental ridgepole. The buildings are low, not many skyscrapers as P. points out because of the earthquake possibility and she reminds me of Frank Lloyd Wright's waiter with the tray idea. Getting out of jet lag into "time" now. Thinking a lot of sex, literal sensation. Plastic food in the windows image for each meal. I like the narrow streets with all kinds of small shops with the talk close like the long last-night stroll with P. after a meal in the "0, 0" Building

Orient last night before and after supper and remember "information" with new "Sony Nude" plugs in ear stereo surface to skin technology also the multi bright colours and green sheen rooftop tiles futons hung flagged on balconies for wind and sunny day and in a lineup her clean flat and shining black hair in front of me is so far away distant untouchable strange that should be

Aug 4
Get from Tokyo to Narita airport then to Seoul, Taipei, and Hong Kong. Now wait in airport transit lounge in Taiwan for flight to continue. In Cantonese language territory I feel more comfortable with an exhibit of beautiful mainland calligraphy, painting, and ceramics brought over by Chiang. Western piano music. I watch a bald-headed nun or monk and dark ethnic Chinese, maybe Tibetan. P. reads a novel by Patrick White, goof plot, she says. Eyes tired from what, body just tired.

Is that Chopin with the waxed evening light people me looking so hard for something to connect with sounds or faces an image out of all my images story unknown building blocks from then to now tangent to hearing a rhythm without having to pay attention to the melody?

Aug 5
We tour Hong Kong today in a bus with a guide hyping photos of ourselves. I start taking notes re: places I've seen my father since he died. I think of him here in this city, in transit, sixty years ago. See first statues and full of colour (white is death, why Ethel didn't want a white coffin for him, red for marriage) numbers too, 9 for longevity and active life, 8 for wealth (there it is, the 8-spot lottery Grampa's gambling smile confirmed).

Numbers in everything said
        clatter each block commerce tooled
fronted with "making" some piece or all of it
        "lucre" personal contrivance shuttle
family woven decades ahead first
        his father and even him and his son
place attribute magnetic magic
        machined into tailored jade street single
attempt to move made so that "generation" gets
        skyline to 1997 after direct incant from
latitude Cantonese genocide nil hope stalled not
        to edit out immigrant identity cancel
head count not really meaningful money exchange
        added up with calculation mind counts the years
abacus clicks in the market stall can't wait
        or seasonal switch typhoon number late
afternoon maybe a winter somewhere in his mind
        but far away, far away.

Aug 8
In Canton (Guangzhou) now after train ride out from Hong Kong. I see my father everywhere. I realize he was only four years old when he arrived in China.

You would have had to learn Cantonese
just as you acquired Canadian prairie world view age four.
Must have hurt to have to find new boyhood lingo
(so silence)
then at twenty-two to relearn English Swift Current
Elite Cafe sufficiency. What tax on your life
left you with all that angry language world inside
and from China too (silent)

There is all this tangibility to my life here, things I can touch base with. I don't let myself feel "foreign" here, even with my funky expectations of their political life that I find so mysterious. I look at the red soldiers in the train station with awe, and the workers in the streets become some sort of generalization about themselves from the real imagination, e.g., the streets are full of "masses." But the person is what one aces so this is exactly where I should pay attention to "ontogeny."

Don't let valour go with the name chiefly
in the accumulated value of the family a prize
within the state strength is bondless unless
the heart carries this calculated boldness outside
to exude many such indications about ourselves
such as the relative colour inside of me or inside of you.

So what have I got going besides this "father" list? I watched a painter leaned over the table doing calligraphy last night, watched him, watched his body, looked for his "chi" rising to the surface, quick, flashy, very intentional moves, so the flurry of the brush was true. I like the actualization of the intent that was not an intent an inclination, really, a bent or a "tropos" which was paid attention to. Me. I've misplaced the family information my mother gave me so I can't check out actual possible connections still here in the Canton region. I mention this to the guides and the others in our tour group, tell them my father was sent here as a child to be raised and educated by his Chinese relatives.

You were part Chinese, I tell them.
They look at me. I'm pulling their leg.
So I'm Chinese too and that's why my name is Wah.
They don't really believe me. That's okay.
When you're not "pure" you just make it up.

From Hong Kong on (to Guangzhou, which used to be Canton, fly to Zhengzhou, then by train north to Taiyuan, Datong, and Hohhot, and finally Beijing) I saw my father everywhere. Notes of these sightings resulted in the following prose extract.

About a year after you died I saw you. You were alone in a car and passed me going the other way. You didn't look at me. Over the past fifteen years this has happened maybe once or twice a year. I'll catch a glimpse of you on a street corner, disappearing through a doorway, or gesturing to someone in the booth of a Chinese cafe. What always gives you away is your haircut, your walk, or the flash in your eyes. You haven't seemed to notice me or ever said anything to me. In China your appearances were overwhelming.

One morning you were doing tai chi in a park near our hotel in Kowloon. I saw the side of your head and the steadfastness of your face as you moved through the classic Grasp the Sparrow's Tail. You wore a white sleeveless undershirt and khaki shorts, sandals, and your brush cut was shorter than usual. It was quite early and very hot and humid. I watched you for a few minutes, from a distance. Your technique seemed forceful and you did your forms alone, out in the open.

After that I knew I would have some strong sensation of you in Canton. The very first morning on the street in front of our hotel I saw you riding your bicycle in the large crowd of bicycles that stream into town from the outskirts every morning. You had something in your mouth, scowl on your face, head down in private thought. Your face has always been very animated and usually says something. Later that same morning I caught a brief glimpse of you through the window of a roadside eatery gesticulating emotionally to someone across from you with your chopsticks. Your body still moves with emphasis and decision. I was quite excited about seeing you so frequently that day.

We visited a commune about 20 km outside Canton and I could imagine you and your sister Ethel working in the rice fields and living in this same small village when you were a boy. As I stepped into a courtyard I saw you ride by on a bicycle, again with a frown on your face. I could tell you were very concerned about something.

During the trip I saw you often and, curiously, more so as we went north. Near the Yellow River you looked so relaxed as you leaned out the window of a truck being loaded with red bricks, enjoying your cigarette. I recognized your stocky frame as you bent to plant your fist of rice shoots in a field just outside Zhengzhou. Whether you were pushing your bike up a hill in the late afternoon in Taiyuan or walking briskly along the street in a coal-mining town in Shensi it was always your black crewcut hair that most stood out.

Perhaps it was only the insinuation of youth from your ruddy cheeks but here in northern China you became younger and the redness of your complexion became more pronounced. To me you had always been older and now suddenly I was the older and watched you through this slick time warp.

You are a father
I am a son and a father
and you were a son
so

I finally realized the full "truth" of these meetings at the Buddhist caves near Datong. There is a temple and a courtyard there, in front of the caves. I was about to leave and on a path alongside a wall you walked past me going the other way and brushed my arm. Yes, brushed. I could see it was intentional and our eyes met for an instant as you turned and glanced over the head of the baby boy you were carrying. Though you didn't say anything your face still talked to me.

Aug 10
Flying into Zhengzhou – stomach last night – turquoise on C.A.A.C. Trident plane. Over rice paddies again – incessant agriculture wherever possible – huge river plains – symmetry of fields and irrigation channels – clouds – I look for the voice – what has happened to colour – now her voice comes over the P.A., about to land, etc. – the nine tones of Cantonese the four tones of Mandarin.

When they plant the rice they bend their backs over and
fall into the sky of the water they look at all day long
look for extension out to other geographical scenes roots
and fist down in the mud dream of green large human
connection a terrain to give colour to the water and the
place table it

Friday, Aug 13
In Taiyuan. Arrived yesterday after tiring all-night-long train ride from Zhengzhou. Yakked late into the night with the other men, some of their racist preconceptions seeping in to take over the experience. Jumbled and noisy dreams through the train tracks. I find the tour demanding physically as well so I haven't been doing much writing but even this morning in the hotel I find the writing very relaxing, dialogue set up with mind. I try the old-fashioned pen nib and ink that is supplied in our room – stop to go to the inkwell to get more ink with school days memory synapse that allows the mind to gather the cloud head of thinking residue and push it out, every strand. The writing during the day has no form or direction, just Father notes. I've been reading Paul Engle's edition of Mao's poems, good with lots of background notes, so I have some of that floating around as I look, and look, and look.

The Answer to "Where is the official Tao Yuan-ming?" in Mao's poem "Ascent of Lu Mountain"

He's not plowing the field by "The Peach Blossom Spring."
It's August, the heat is too much
it shimmers the bushes,
and he, too, dreams of the oceans.
He's gone, took to the sky river like a father,
sells Laoshan mineral water late at night
on a train to Kokanee Glacier.

Aug 14
The caves at Datong were a central feature of our journey and it is at about this time when the following prose poem was written.

You are me on a train going north through central China. I don't think you've been here before; I haven't. You hold out a green flag at the rear of the train. Then I see you lounging on top of a pile of hemp rope on the station platform and you look in through the train window, at me. After the train starts to roll I watch you look out in quietude at the countryside. As the sun sets over the loess hills you look for remains of the Great Wall on the distant broken ridges. There is a red star on your hat. Strangers come up to you and ask questions in a foreign language. That lights up your eyes. I think of the house you live in on the Mongolian border with its south-facing door painted bright yellows, oranges, and reds. You hardly ever think of that door but the image is quickly accessible to you and when you talk to a fellow worker, a comrade, in your own language, the colours of the door imbue your conversation. As the train pulls into a station in the early evening darkness you disappear.

A couple of days later, in the caves at Datong, you think you recognize one of the statues, a bodhisattva with leg bent at the knee. It reminds you of one of your parents but you can't tell why or which one. Your parents, as you remember them, have become one just as you were once one in their married mind. An attempt to separate their image into two separate people won't work. They are now one in the image of this statue and this coalescence reminds

you of the singularity of origins, of the primary, the
fundamental, and that makes good sense to you, that
somewhere in this stone religion you would find something
of yourself. It is this very reflection of oneself in things
that accounts for you and I intersecting at this moment.
For example, the incredibly brilliant eight-hundred-year-old paint on
the statues here reminds you of lapis and the depth you
feel akin to in that rock, though I remember you were
always hot on jade, more cultural than personal I think.
As you sit in the warmth of the August morning sun and
write this you have attracted a large crowd of Chinese
who stop to watch the language flow out onto the paper.
You look up at them and ask them in English if they would
like to write something on your paper but they simply
smile and ignore you. They are more interested in the
writing and comment to one another and point to the
actual incisions you make on the paper, the calligraphy
of the foreign letters cutting also into their minds as they
recognize something of themselves there. When you think
about it all sorts of connections are lost.

Sometime later that day, on the hotel steps, you and I are
two old men smoking cigarettes and listening to the jarring
brass gongs of a Chinese opera on the radio. They just
look into one another's eyes. The gong usually signals a
movement onstage.

Monday, August ?
We travel all day out to the Inner Mongolian grasslands in a small passenger van. Through the bus window I catch yet another glimpse of "you."

You might have been this guy in Hohhot – one room, one
rooster – or is my skin bone brown so singular and
contained in China eyes deep within the common view
connected so that I see what you saw sometimes just to
stand in the doorway with creosote eyes imprint death
(too, maybe) but certainly to experience any complete
person living there is always a mirror how alone can one be?

In the late afternoon we arrive and I sit and look out of a yurt at the beautiful landscape of long, flat, rolling plateau and prairie horizon. A herd of camels brushes the camp and then moves faster than we can run into the distance. There's a lovely flush on the Mongolian girls' cheeks which is very attractive. Someone says it's from dairy products and outdoor living. I think of pudeur.

The blush / flush shy guilt blood rush sign that is the origin of colour from the inner heat we rush outward (other animals don't blush do they?) these girls sing for us shrill voices behind the heat in their cheeks like in my family when they drink or the love of my daughters too in their first flush / first guilt so red something of *The Scarlet Letter* is why J.C. pointed to the story as the truth which rises from some depth sensation feeling the deep heat in the parts of the body move and make yourself so red which tells the story the telltale blush of revelation we are.

Tuesday
Raining this morning but now the sun is out. We visited a yurt house and had some great yogourt. It's made straight from milk without boiling; they leave fresh milk sit for two or three days so actually it becomes sour cream but this wasn't sour. Too much riding on our bus through the countryside these last few days. Images of our trip, the terrain, and P.

Hue of loess August terrace planted green and heavy water
then yellow dry by mid-September our marriage wanders
again through the millennia of marriages here in the earth
brush your knee on the bus, think of the caves, the yolk
of an egg, the rice.

Friday the 20th August in Beijing
Touring the city. Lotus fields everywhere. Look at the hats they wear. Everything happiness and longevity.

At the Summer Palace the peach
the symbol of lucre
each picture different
from the classics
5,000 – no repetition

Or everywhere, the masses, the people from New York airing their teeth. I think to try to get to the particular, the minute, underneath the lushness of the ornamental, the specific (therefore simple?), rediscover "decoration" as useful, function.

The words for the things
    are not the things themselves
    of course

Mao's mausoleum, now the Great Hall of the People. When we walked into the large room just before seeing his body I was struck by the very large painting of the mountains along one wall because of a poem I had written years ago as I looked out over the mountains along the Kootenay River from our house.

Mao, in front of me
the things you cared for too

river, mountain
a town, the whole
blue sky.

(FROM)

Waiting for Saskatchewan

(1985)

ELITE

(pronounced *ee-light*)

ELITE 1

Swift Current, Saskatchewan, is at the centre. I don't think you were a boy there. Probably what happened is your family moved there from Medicine Hat just before you were four, just before you and Ethel were sent to China. I know all these "facts" existed once, and I could check some of them out with Ethel, or your other sisters and brothers, Buster, Lil, Flo, Jimmy. But, like the information on distant relatives I lost just before going into China, somehow I don't want it or need it. The facts seem partially unreal. Anyway, you must have seen Swift Current just before Grampa put you on the train. About 1916. I was driving across the Prairies on New Year's Eve last year and we decided to stop for the night in Swift Current. It was close to midnight and so we thought we'd welcome in the new year in a pub downtown. I hadn't been there for over thirty years but I felt natural in following Central Avenue to the old train station. As soon as I saw the station I knew just where I was. I stopped the car and pointed out to Pauline the exact spot I stood when the war was over and I met you at the station when you came home from training camp. From there the lay of the land was clear to me. There was Roy's shoe shop and just up the street across from Woolworths was the Elite Cafe You were always there, in the Elite, working. I remember the streets more on my own. Not just the photographs, but me walking, alone in the town. Touching a building, the flowerpots in Mother Trimble's windowsills, the cool shade under some outside stairway, etc. I never talked to you about these things, even when they weren't memories. They weren't really important at the time. Your memory of such particulars. Mine. Does it matter? The reason for the story is simply to count on it. What I remember or what you or anyone else connected remembers isn't the point. There isn't even any point. There is just this. You, before you had a car, on the street in an overcoat, winter, to work. Always alone. I mean I see only your singularity, you with hands in your pockets, head down, going to work, with intention, in the cold winter dusk, to the Elite, your dad or Buster already has the big stainless steel coffee urn ready, what was it, twenty cups of ground in the cloth sack and, what, the first few customers, not farmers, you can't even speak English at first, silence, from China too, sweep the floors, maybe do some cooking in the kitchen where you can talk to the cooks, Grampa out front flipping coins, the whole family around you there in Swift Current, your new old family, by then silence and anger hum, alone.

ELITE 2

Do you remember how living on the Prairies was like living in water, in an ocean or a large lake. Movements, decisions, fortunes were made by undercurrent, a sense of sliding along a large floor, in the night. The night I was with you on a trip, just before we moved out to B.C., it felt like that, the way we moved, probably by train, through unknown territory. Always you had an "intent." You were on business of some sort and the others we met were all Chinese. You could talk to them. They gave me candy and pinched me. You and they talked and talked. Chinese always sounds so serious, emotional, angry. I napped on a couch in some Chinese store in some Alberta town. The old men played dominoes and smoked and drank tea. In the window dusty plants in porcelain bowls and some goldfish. Does it seem strange to you now to see this in words? Do you remember the trip I'm talking about? Late at night somewhere you played mah jong. From outside the sound of the click-clack of the pieces being shuffled over the tabletop under the hum of the men's voices, a real music I felt comfortable with. Even though you stayed late you always came back, going somewhere. We moved that night through this subcontinent of prairie landscape, it was summer and the water was warm and hazy, the possible distances, distant.

ELITE 3

I'm on the Prairies this winter. I haven't been here in the winter since I was four years old. It's not Swift Current, or Speedy Creek as some here call it, but there are certain flavours that are unmistakably part of us. The ethnicity here feels so direct. I mean the Chinese are still connected to China, the Ukrainians so Ukrainian, in the bar the Icelanders tell stories about Iceland, the Swede still has an accent, the French speak French. Here you're either a Wiebe or a Friesen, or not. What is a Metis, anyway? I know when you came back from China you must have felt more Chinese than anything else. But I remember you saying later that the Chinese didn't trust you and the English didn't trust you. You were a half-breed, Eurasian. I remember feeling the possibility of that word "Eurasian" for myself when I first read it in my own troubled adolescence. I don't think you ever felt the relief of that exotic identity though. In North America white is still the standard and you were never white enough. But you weren't pure enough for the Chinese either. You never knew the full comradeship of an ethnic community. So you felt single, outside, though you played the game as we all must. To be a mix here on the Prairies is still noticed. I remember going into Macleods in Swift Current a few years ago and sensing that most of the women in the store were just like Granny Erickson. I don't think you felt there was anyone else in the world like you.

You got us involved in the Salvation Army because that's what Granny Wah wanted. She had a bonnet. I can't recall ever seeing Grampa or you there. But I bet she had her go at you too. Didn't you ever play the big bass drum, or the cymbals? I played the E-flat horn later in Nelson. I think, like Grampa, you always thought the Salvation Army people outside yourself. That was the Chinese in you. You didn't outwardly really trust it. But you tried it. In some totally pure and personal way you prayed, alone. I know later when our family went to the United Church in Nelson and you sometimes got off work on Sunday morning to go to church with us you did sing the hymns but your brow furled as if you couldn't understand the words. You were proud, then, of the fact you were going to church and you made a point of telling some of the customers in the restaurant that you had to go to church. That was after you had stopped desiring China and the Chinese at work put up with but laughed at you going to church. I think the church thing was white respectability and you did it for that and a sense of our family in that community. Somehow, in the face of all the Salvation Army, Granny, community, etc., I know you established some real spiritual communication, totally private, no drums.

ELITE 5

There is no picture (or is there) of me leaning over the boards of the Swift Current arena with you there, on the ice in your big overcoat, suit and tie, spiffy, smiling at the camera, and the whole Swift Current Indians (they weren't real "Indians" – that was their name) hockey team working out, swirling big as life over the dark ice. There is a team picture I know. Like the Toronto Maple Leafs hockey calendars that used to hang in the barbershop, the team lined up on the real ice of the Gardens against the backboards. But in this one it's the Indians. I think you were the manager or something, you helped out. The brim of your hat is turned down, Chicago-gangster style. The Indian on their sweaters is just like the Chicago Black Hawks. Strangely Chicago figured in your life. You told us that you ran away from home when they brought you back from China and got work on a boat in the Great Lakes. You jumped ship in Chicago and they picked you up for illegal entry. You were sent back to Swift Current and that was the end of that. I wish you had given us more details. Chicago has always been a mysterious place for me and someday I'll get there myself. Anyway, isn't it strange how that city is there in our lives, on the periphery.

I've always been "proud" you were part of that team. The Swift Current Indians were my first hockey heroes and their movements over the ice instilled a sense of body and mindset that I have carried with me all my life. Even though you never played hockey I know you had the invisible movement of the game inside you too. You said you played basketball on a winning team in China. But you liked hockey. There is no picture, either, of me and my first pair of skates, double runners, with Mom (you were working), on a blustery day, natural ice, on a pond or creek. Or the skating rink you made for us in our backyard in Trail. Or the puck that caught me just above the eye, third row as you and I watched a game in the Civic Centre, blood and stitches. The game on television now, you'd fall asleep before the end of the first period. Did you ever ride a horse?

Line going deep into the lake or flung out onto the surface glaze river current, layers of darkness, invisible fish. You would look at me with serious brown eyes sometimes like I was crazy when I caught a fish and then give your own mad laugh. Something got to you fishing in the Columbia River at Trail, after work, along the rocks, swift-flowing mind emptying, maybe. Or in a creek at Meadow on a Sunday afternoon picnic, cousins and uncles, a ball game. At Apex you driving the road in the turquoise Ford looking for us fishing along the slow meandering of Cottonwood Creek. You without me at Trout Lake. Me without you below the C.P.R. tracks below Granite Road on the way out of town or jigging for suckers near the boathouses with the old Chinaman. When I fish now sometimes I feel like I'm you, water, glassy gaze, vertical, invisible layers, the line, disappearing.

ELITE 7

The dream "noises" of the early morning. You getting ready to go to work, still dark at 4:30, a light dust of snow maybe, the house warm, as you dress, the gabardine pants, shoes I shined for you last night, muffled voices of goodbye, the small change in your pocket, car keys, your pace on the varnished maple floor, alone, quickens with movements towards the door, out, dark-grey mist hackle across the lake on Elephant Mountain, you and the town get going for the day, I hear the blue two-door Pontiac hum alive down on the street, and you're gone to work, and then our own half-awake silence and relaxation back into the morning's warmth and sleep. Or me a couple times a year getting up for you, e.g., Father's Day, some Sunday morning, could you really sleep "in" thinking of me the kid making the big urn of coffee, turning the heat up, remembering to get the cream and a tray of butter out of the cooler, turn on the sign, the synchromesh of everything starting to work, darkness breaking on Baker Street, first customers and the regulars early-morning old-man risers C.P.R. night shift and a few foremen and loners first coffee and cigarettes, the new noises of the day picking up speed and humming along the counter and booths to the whack of the kitchen door kicked on stride and the smells then.

I try to "place" you and the hand or head can't, try to get you into my mountains for example but your China youth and the images of place for you before you were twenty are imbued with the green around Canton rice fields, humid Hong Kong masses – I can't imagine what your image of the world was, where you were in it (were you always going home to Swift Current, were you ever at home, anywhere). How much did you share of how small or large the world was after we left the Prairies – Trail, Nelson, Cranbrook, Calgary, Vancouver? That "reward" of a real holiday down the Columbia and then up the coast to Vancouver when you sold a share in the Diamond Grill. A few trips to Spokane, hikes into the hills around Nelson for fishing, the gravelly drive to Trail and back. Did any shape of such places ever displace the distancing in your eyes? You looked out at it all but you never really cared if you were there or elsewhere. I think you were prepared to be anywhere. The sun, the warmth, was something you went outside for, outside yourself, stretching and relaxing your working moving body, inside, inside, you never betrayed any imprint of a "world" other than your dark-brown eyes.

ELITE 9

When you returned from China via Victoria on Hong Kong Island and they put you in jail in Victoria on Vancouver Island because your birth certificate had been lost in the Medicine Hat City Hall fire and your parents couldn't prove you were born in Canada until they found your baptism records in the church or in the spring of 1948 when we moved to Nelson from Trail during the floods while Mao chased Chiang Kai-shek from the mainland to offshore Taiwan and the generalissimo's picture hung in our house and on a wall above some plants and goldfish in the Chinese Nationalist League house down on Lake Street or when you arrived in China in 1916 only four years old unable to speak Chinese and later in the roaring twenties when each time Grampa gambled away your boat passage so you didn't get back to Canada until 1930 languageless again with anger locked up in the immigration cells on Juan de Fuca Strait or when your heart crashed so young at fifty-four as you fell from Mom's arms to the dance floor did you see islands?

ELITE 10

Your father owned the Regal across from the railway station but you worked in the Elite on Central Avenue right next to the Venice and the Paris was the one on the corner all three across the street from Cooper's store where Connie worked in the dry goods department after school and then full-time after graduation the year you took her to the final basketball game at Gull Lake and Mom says now you borrowed a car and drove to Moose Jaw for a honeymoon and bought your first house in Swift Current in the fall of 1939 for nine hundred dollars just after I was born and Connie's dad fixed it up so you sold it and bought another, stucco (I remember that one) in '41 then moved to Trail in the spring of '43 and bought the Expert Cleaners and sold it to Andy's brother Sam and his wife and bought a house there on a corner right across from the river near Butler ballpark by the bridge and the next one where we had our first dog it was down closer to Sandy Beach where Granny and Grampa lived at the foot of Sandy Mountain and then Ernie's dog Mickey up in the house in the next block to the Dollar Cleaners all in east Trail while you and Grampa were in the Elite across the river downtown underneath the smelter hill and then in the spring of '48 floods when we moved to Nelson didn't you and Jimmy Gee Ethel's husband buy into the L.D. Cafe which you changed to the New Star just as Mao's victory north of the Yangtze became palpable and we lived in the duplex with the oil stove at 314 Carbonate before you got into your last restaurant (and mine) the Diamond Grill which even with the Standard down by

Hipperson's Hardware times got good on Baker Street in the fifties and you got Grampa Erickson to build us our own house with maple floors at 724 Victoria you were so proud we had fireworks for the housewarming and two sittings for the Chinese banquet in the basement and finally the Holmes Motel in Cranbrook in the early sixties where that was the end of the deals the cafes the houses the driving the building the running right through it, for you, that was it.

THIS DENDRITE MAP:
FATHER/MOTHER HAIBUN

FATHER/MOTHER HAIBUN 1

Finally changed the calendar today to August. Sitting here this morning trying to figure out things (phone rings and she asks, "Is this David? I must have the wrong number. I don't know why I keep doing this.") the *ecrit* I'm open for, ungular, now alone in the mornings looking through Jung and Hillman for hints, I mean the simple and solid clarity of my father's father's dying, his dying, and then me living and then dying too is outrageous, bald as geographical Saskatchewan and my grandfather which made my life "radical" not that he actually came to be there but simply him here/there and her, my grandmother, her Salvation Army Scottishness really solid in the middle of his flux but both of them cutting "geo" out of their world thus Maple Creek Moose Jaw North Battleford Medicine Hat somewhere in England and Canton, China, places in their lives much more than in their world, you, my father, almost too, thus me, such particles caught in the twig-jam holding the water back impedimenta and this dendrite map I'm finally on now for no reason but time, and then I'll go to the city and look for an S-shaped chair to rock me into each day.

Two weeks late
I turn the calendar
crave for ripe tomatoes

FATHER/MOTHER HAIBUN 2

Anger the same thing as you behind my face, eyes, maybe. A larger-than-usual black bear, eating, high up in the thin wild cherry trees in the gully this morning, sun just coming up. I peer around the corner of the garage at the bear just like you would, eyes squinted brow lined in suspicion like yours used to, as if you were trying to figure out something serious. I feel your face in me like that sometimes, looking out of me, and now I wonder if my anger is the same as yours flying out of me from him and his, etc., the anger molten back through chthonic fear. The bear flushed off, finally, by the dog. You hover in the cool August morning air, behind my eyes. The fire, the candle, the pumpkin, the "virtu," inside.

Crash of broken branch
hungry
pits in the shit

FATHER/MOTHER HAIBUN 3

I try talking to you in this near-September air after I water the dry spots out of the lawn, morning sunny and clear the air coming to this for months ahead, almost, your death month, turning the flowers, even those huckleberries I picked yesterday had thoughts of the frost ahead high in the mountains, such simple weather but something more primitive here pictures of the kids each year on the first day of school in front of the flowers in their new clothes, ahead, you too and my mind working over the connections, you're laughing, skeptical, like when I told you they used hot water to make the ice at the arena because it steams and you just about believed it because I did, my heart shoots into the memory of that actual mouths-and-eyes-talking dialogue, weather is memory every time I wonder if you ever really listened to the songs on the Wurlitzer in the cafe, particularly on a quiet winter Sunday afternoon, the words anytime your mind roaming ahead and behind like mine the little shots at living each day all the things air carries for thinking just like that.

Music
I try to think of the words to "Autumn Leaves"
"Love Letters in the Sand"

FATHER/MOTHER HAIBUN 4

Your pen wrote Chinese and your name in a smooth swoop with flourish and style, I can hardly read my own tight scrawl, could you write anything else, I know you could read, nose in the air and lick your finger to turn the large newspaper page pensively in the last seat of those half-circle Arborite counters in the Diamond Grill, your glasses case bulging your shirt pocket with that expensive pen, always a favourite thing to handle the way you treated it like jewellery, actually it was a matched pen and pencil set, Sheaffer maybe (something to do with Calgary here), heavy, silver, black, gold nib, the precision I wanted also in things, that time I conned you into paying for a fountain pen I had my eye on in Benwell's stationery store four dollars and twenty cents Mom was mad but you understood such desires in your cheeks relaxed when you worked signing cheques and doing the books in the back room of the cafe late at night or how the pen worked perfectly with your quick body as you'd flourish off a cheque during a busy noon-hour rush the sun and noise of the town and the cafe flashing.

High muckamuck's gold-toothed clicks
ink mark red green on lottery blotting paper
8-spot (click-click)

FATHER/MOTHER HAIBUN 5

You can't drive through a rainbow I said hills to myself in the mountains glory of a late-summer early-fall thunderstorm the Brilliant Bluffs brilliant indeed the shine rain and sunshine waves of science breaking lickety-split school systems memory for the next word after colour from the other side no one could see it otherwise nature's path is home to the bluebird triangular son/event/father w/ time-space China rainbow over your youth vertical like on the Prairies that rainbow stood straight up into the sky on the horizon you'd think in the winter sun ice crystals could form unbelievable.

> Radio on, up north
> an American hunter shoots a rare white moose
> geese in the sky, nibbling ribbons

FATHER/MOTHER HAIBUN 6

I wish you were alive here in my life so we could share the ease of our lives growing older together, now time would catch up with the gap of our ages, 45–72, ethnicity would be gone, just skin and the winding down, the fence Jenefer & I built along the back, hockey games, the sunny fall day, this sentimentalism, songs too, like crazy white American jukebox "Mule Train" in your imagination I thought just as those events are in mine, no, but you and the Great Lakes boats desire, absolutely your own, undying care for the single, your own world fact, all this buffer, as down the road in the village from us this so-called community, the ones we care for really spread over the whole earth if possible, padding of the family too, this softness around ourselves so that we want it, so common we could talk about it now, but so alone, so alone.

I'll stain the fence red
a dim border in the snow
might last thirty years

FATHER/MOTHER HAIBUN 7

I was back in Buffalo when you died and when I came out for your funeral at the end of September there was snow on Elephant Mountain as far down as Pulpit Rock from Ernie's house the lake quiet my mother alone suddenly, months unused, unusual, I knew you best in the winter when there was curling and hockey or in the summer when we fished, dark mornings on the way to work or wet leaves in the gutter, driving at this time of year from Cranbrook to Nelson for the Lions dance, car heater toasty-warm upholstery, outside the air wet and cool mist hackles in the mountains your life simply closing down in the quiet month on the Hume Hotel ballroom floor wobble of the planet's sun seasons shortened golden flower's corny harvest elixir completed.

Road's nearly empty
only a few pickups
with firewood

FATHER/MOTHER HAIBUN 8

The pulse. So. When I take it now the microsystem wild card is almost cellular in its transport of the image imprint forward or I think back pictures. Some Saturday afternoons I'd have to take off work at the Diamond to play soccer down at the Civic, or you'd feed me a steak before a midget hockey bus trip to Trail, after the game Frenchie's French fries outside the Cominco, my earth my world which grosses more sensation, you knew more than I did, now my daughter has grown up into her stomach too, large encryptic sublease a full-grown symptom of I'm just curious about this body. You read it all, playing games is really not such a big deal but I always thought I had to pad it a bit to get off work, the world and out the door down the street, you knew it and me, outside the sun and the chemicals it's either numbers or that large kicked and swinging wooden door.

Felled tree in the fall
I look at the stump for sap
zero

"Why do you think of your father so much?"

"He's dead. Every once in a while I think I see him, or someone I see reminds me of him, or I'm writing this book and he's in it."

"That's not the truth. There's more to it than that."

"What we'll try for is a paradigm in this."

"You can think of a fishing cause. For him environment is connected with the earth."

"Dante phoned last night. From Salmo. And the day before, Mike Zoll showed up and told me, 'The subtle quality of things transcends all formal boundaries.' I don't know, I'm not sure, maybe."

"Do women think a circle is a labyrinth?"

"Kore, no one wears purple like you. I half expect you to come with a hat."

"I feel I'm lucky I'm part Chinese when I see a river."

"So. What about your father?"

"Look, it's an old problem. When Smaro says, "Alley alley home free," I know exactly what's going on. Her eyes twinkle. Here, it's snowing today. Sounds are deadened, like waking up in a room with the windows closed. Why do you ask?"

"'Autumn in New York,' 'Moonlight in Vermont,' they're all haiku. And that's just one of the tricks Lionel knows. You know that poem about his dad and the echo of the axe on the other side of the valley? That was in the fall, there was frost. Or Victor's poem, 'Kenkyusha: Day Nine,' his daughter's birth, my father's death, zooming in on the phoneme of time, accurate, and asks me, 'What time.'"

"You'd better ask Peter about Jack Clarke's Hegel's 'discipline of service and obedience' and 'the lake Fred Wah said it all ends up in' in case McNaughton and the hidden *d* can help."

"Maybe tomorrow. I've been carrying it around all week. It's the epitaph to my Aunt Hannah's grave in Swift Current. It's like a song. Whenever I think of it I can hear my Granny Wah singing, front row, in the Salvation Army hall, and I can see her grey-blue eyes softened with a bit of surprise."

Hannah Elizabeth
fell asleep in Jesus Arms
1918–1936

FATHER/MOTHER HAIBUN 10

Working with my back to the window for more natural light, dog chasing cows in the field, the words stubble today, embedded there in the bracken at the edge of the field, Chinese philosophy and numbers, the cloud-filled night, "and they swam and they swam, right over the dam," etc., all this, and sugar too, holding the hook, time, the bag, the book, the shape, you also carried on your back yin and embraced yang with your arms and shoulders, the mind as a polished mirror, there, back into my hand.

> I can't stop looking
> at the field of brown grass and weed
> and feeling the grey sky

FATHER/MOTHER HAIBUN 11

Mother somewhere you flying over me with love and close careless caress from Sweden your soft smooth cream skin only thoughts from your mother without comparison the lightness of your life/blood womanness which is mine despite language across fetalness what gods of northern europe bring out of this sentence we say and live in outside of the wife of the storm god's frictive battle with the "story" our names.

> Rain washes first snow
> old words here on the notepad
> "Where did Odysseus go?"

FATHER/MOTHER HAIBUN 12

Mom, you'll know this as a word game, strategy to get truth's attention, your name, Corrine, for example, core, cortex, heart, blood, islands of the liver, a tension to incite the present, your friend Woody written into the texture, coloured uphill under their apple tree beautiful also, we were about fifteen when Wayne Waters said to me, "Your mother's a good-looking woman" and I blushed, tissue of skin, shades of other people's hair, touch.

> The landscape is red
> *pudeur*
> an air of sanctity and respect

FATHER/MOTHER HAIBUN 13

The issue is to divide into two, duplicate, derive language which is a filter for the blood, and then to replenish thought in a precise flow to converge again on life, how much a copy of you I am also a material for my own initials (F.J.) Karen Marie Erickson when your mother died all the undoubling condensed memory added up to a single snowy winter month as January.

I get up and look
no sky today, just the fog.
How one can one be?

FATHER/MOTHER HAIBUN 14

When my hands, arms, and head grew larger there was at one point a very warm sensation which I thought might relate to my birth when sometimes you rub your wrist joints this spherical map of "influence" as in Dad's anger, maybe, or you clear your throat that's when I wait for simply old age and a mental space serrated description narrative the same female song a refrain for the fictive or theory that there is in vocation the gift of a blueprint.

In winter ravens look more majestic
weaving over the highway
tree to tree, tree to tree

FATHER/MOTHER HAIBUN 15

All this imaging is only the subliminal daily cache because of your first real house on Second Avenue and the *Just Mary* show time with you in the radio air of the room carpet *Journeys Through Bookland* "Tom and the Water-Babies" with story every morning and on Sunday afternoons got "serial" eyes with *Jake and the Kid* or John Drainie's story hour quiet spring evenings Sergeant Drake on the Vancouver waterfront breathing radio-world innuendo a mother with secrets when the snow blows in circles over the farms final connections to the ancient world.

Someday I'll grow them
prairie hollyhocks again
on a stucco wall

FATHER/MOTHER HAIBUN 16

I know the language just turns you into metaphor, rock of ages like Granny Wah, the truth. Traces of the other mothers, cliff dwellers in the golden city, your windows' nothingness to the world's something, bison on the walls at Lascaux. So there. How to defend you and me from a language edited by Christians I stand facing west with my father and speak words which are new names for the sea.

> Old month's countenance
> deer swim the rock-wall river
> mean anything to you?

FATHER/MOTHER HAIBUN 17

O Mother, the brightness of the birch tree's bark in this November mid-afternoon sunset, fringes, the datum which is permanent, the external events of all that stuff actual energy is created from, you on a different planar syntax Jenefer discovers in turning the yin/yang key, a cyclic thing going on there, ontologic principle, all the daughters want it, one pot, this morning I watered your Christmas cactus bursting brilliant pink and purple on schedule for your birthday again, and you should see Helen's what'd those philosophers say, he beats the drum, he stops, he sobs, he sings – they had mothers.

> You flew over me
> outside there was a moist loss
> now I remember

FATHER/MOTHER HAIBUN 18

I'd say that's a "proud" or swollen wound on my finger, body's pride to remind itself of itself, something genitive about the blue sloped roof of the '51 Pontiac, lives broken into car eras, both of you (thus us) the heat on the edge of healing skin, red, something Eucharistic and my own two daughters even this spring, fall leeched ground and then outside the flowers see how hard it is for me to make sense of a hunch, looking around myself, looking for the simple "of" connection might be, such as why my friend Albert set out his amaryllis this spring.

> No more snow to shovel this winter
> back to the ground, flowers
> for all to see

FATHER/MOTHER HAIBUN 19

I'm here alone for the weekend, get fires going and burn all that junk, mind keeps that there to clean up. I get some rice on and the cabin's warm. Now I sit here, sip a beer and dwell on my aloneness, the solitary singleness and being older now. That is a prediction I gave myself when I watched some of the old men around town, isolation. Night falling. Cold over the lake, fingers of clouds in the western sky above Woodbury Creek. I told Peter that's the process I'm interested in as long as I can keep getting the language out. Now I'm as old as you were. The fire outside in the dark comes from your eyes. The words of our name settle down with everything else on this shore.

Smoke sits on the lake
frost tonight
eyes thinking

FATHER/MOTHER HAIBUN 20

I still don't know how to use the chopsticks as right or as natural, bamboo fingers hands arms mind stomach, food steaming off the dishes, rain or wet snow, windows, night lights, small meals you'd grab between rushes (unlike me), that's what you did, isn't it, went back to the cafe later, on the nights we didn't have rice at home, me too, when I first went to university in Vancouver I couldn't stand it, I'd need rice, catch the Hastings bus to Chinatown, what is it, this food business, this hovering over ourselves?

> A little ginger, a little garlic
> black beans, lo bok
> Auntie Ethel, the kitchen

FATHER/MOTHER HAIBUN 21

Speedy dancing and the leaves of Germany meet me at the elevator, words mean everything, I try to phone you on Mother's Day, everyone does, more Swedish than Chinese, you didn't want me to be a Boy Scout all my life, did you (the leaves cling to this writing), sometimes to be battle ready Norbert Ruebsaat, genetics and geographics, he can tell you too, exactly like mother alphabet the new lyric feet, McKinnon's South America eyesight I tell myself my self-perception, palace/place/police, spring leafless trees on Ontario's horizon, did Pindar catch us dead in our tracks?

Japanese plum blossoms
my finger joints swollen, your kind of love
sweetest, get that, sweetest

(FROM *So Far*)

Utaniki

(1991)

Saturday, August 1/87
I talk to myself this morning, on the long drive up the Columbia Valley. I notice that, that I talk to myself more than to others, I say that to myself, that and where we're going, the fresh of the morning, the truck packed with hiking gear, that, and that. Pauline and I meet the others at the Skookumchuk Cafe for the long drive up the gravel logging road valleys, people eyes ahead faces set on the next step, a chopper lift up to 8,000 ft. in the Rockies east of Invermere. But the weather socks in during the day so after I wrap the truck in chicken wire, mezmerize alone, lean on a log long hours but no chopper, unwrap the car and spend the night there, strewn w/ cloud (I hope stars).

This afternoon I unzipped the pocket of my pack and found this journal, left or lost since last summer's hiking camp in Anemone Pass in the northern Selkirks. In it I find this poem I wrote in response to Pat Lifely's fall from a cliff during the first days of that camp.

A Garnet for Pat Lifely

Here's a small encrusted stone for your cairn
home for you.

this wine-red nipple of the January mind
your death fell from
every day we face them
those rock bluffs across the valley, a pine

large alpine sky arches over these slopes each night
oh wonder of rock and water and earth

what alchemical lake we and this are

This then
periodic counting
not-forgotten alpine meadow winter sod
under all this weight of place:

wind too
flowers we've named, snow
patches, ledges, creeks, lakes, marmots, eagles, clouds

and on to the face we glass each day
that bluff between our eyes
lake and the waterfall
                                        striations
of a life
                                simple single
gouge in a rock

Ha!
    have you become our pet cow-bird
    hop for mosquitoes at mealtime?

    is that you, then, already disappeared further south
    w/ the caribou?

This garnet, such a little thing to leave here for you.

But birds have that quick and darting look – they know
winter's coming,
                    that
they don't decide.

The stones of paradise ripen. We pick them up as reminders, touchstones, like the clock of the Big Dipper, filigree of mind set on never sinking below the horizon, or in migration as a way home.

The best ones are found close to treeline or snowline or brow line. Sometimes the line is recognized after the rock's been pocketed, but only with distance.

Lines can be cracks, as in an avalanche.

Sunday
This morning we still wait for the first sound of the chopper in the clouds. Gusty and raining a bit. All day I either sit in the car and work with the words, talk to myself, or walk along the gravel road alone and taste the old work, summer timber cruising.

Years ago nothing in the sky
grey whales of cumulus floated slow all day
at the head of the valley

just another gravel road
    w/ clear-cut rubble down to the creek

Late afternoon over the washboard
pickup truck a trail of dust

or a wet October Sunday
            – all the gravel roads so settled down, quiet
                all alone

Finally, in the late afternoon, the cloud ceiling lifts a bit and the chopper comes through. He gets us in before supper. Tents set up on a small pond-filled bench and we start to feel the spread of place: dewed grass, boots, flashlights, bite of air in the nose.

> Gravel, garnet, granite, seed, tree, mountain – all ones also inescapably in Thoreau's choice of the Milky Way just like every logging road I come across I run over the stardust again until the soul sings *Oh!* or even talking to myself the same old rhythm, breathing but with notice of the weather, the time of day even.

Monday
From the camp we hike up about 1,000 ft. We'll have to do this most days to reach the range of rambling available. I walk along a stunning grey and red limestone highway/arena, huge typochronic wave-swirl of razor rock. Patches of cliff-clinging grass and flowers. Pauline can't understand why I don't get into the names, like "something poisonous something" (elegant poison camas) or fringed grass of Parnassus. So as I walk along talking that one out to myself I figure that naming is more than only counting, that it also works as a very particular image, like Nancy-Jean's "sorrel" up Kokanee, or I'm always looking for saxifrage on the edge of my

eye, that one lonely flower (maybe "mist maiden" or "mountain aben") she called me back up the scree to photograph in Anemone Pass last summer. Yet there is that surface of experience, say, just walking and breathing, e.g., tables of limestone today with little islands of schist sticking up into the Vibram almost like Velcro. But the problem with naming is number. You can't look at, let alone count, all of it.

Like right now after lunch someone yaps "get the maps" and I think of the maps folded up in my pack and how I never really use them for the specific, just an overview (imaginary mostly).

> How easily lost I
> could get

Back in camp I play around with a watercolour card for Liz, the young teenager who hiked with us today.

> The goat.
> She thought.
> She saw.
>
> I think we acquire surfaces of a world and that's what becomes the planar echo or projection called flowering which later could be the ghost-like residue of skin, leaf, or story and other filmed shapes of ceremonial intimacy.

Tuesday

I've spent all day chasing after but never finding the people I started hiking with. They were going around a ridge I hiked up over and I lost them. Everywhere I look – no trace. Disappeared. I've scrambled up a couple of high hills, yelled, yodelled, scanned, and listened to my nervous breath. Now I've sort of given up and had a bath in the ice-cold lakes.

Not lost
Heart beats
Alone
All day
Long

Day all
Alone
Beats heart
Lost not.

To not shout loud enough into the pond is okay, it'll still be there next penetrating some veiled alliance, rephrased portrait, reverse scheme stuck in the throat we depend on to cut into place when needed, hopeless levers of cyclicity sentencing device to sameness so as to clip the cry at the stomach-carving thrust over the lakes and across the valley, still here, mouthing out the cave.

Wednesday
Fingers stiff and cold as I write this because a wet front moved through last night. Mist hackles hang and float so I decide to stay in camp for a few hours and fiddle around with a pinhole camera. Pauline, Liz, and I amble off later on to Waterfall Lake just above us and then to Limestone Lakes where I photograph and paint for an hour.

A picture of shooting star that primrose easy day connections in my body brush chromatic hills and mountains dilute grey those pigments glinted out the corner of cerulean blue above (no black or white) but Winsor green dark burnt umber raw sienna cadmium yellow watered yellow ochre for the lakes the limestone hills and wet blue paper for the sky left o.

Nothing's wrong here. This is the palace. This is the place.

Thursday
Today Pauline and I hike off alone down to Sylvan Pass roundabout but we overshoot height and there we are on a ridge above the pass so the day is really a trial until I realize on the way home we

discover foot ramps of rock and grass down to and up from each wee lake and that sidehilling elk cut across to the ridge before Longview Peak gets us sheer height above what down below five foreign backpackers cut across the grey and red amphitheatre. From there we make plans for home. Down on the limestone floor we sit on the lip of a huge sinkhole river rumbling hundreds of feet beneath and after that the trip back's a maze of diagonals along the arcades finally down to a lake to swim and bathe and by mistake find our way out again.

Ancient ochre valley
hosts rock events
but the elk find human trails around everything.

Trust those trails
and we won't get any more lost
than all of us already are.

Subterranean river tracking the needed code recognizes tulle of ocean/desert reflective saying animal palm's line earth outer voice radioed position echoing in on carbon some seed still packed with palace so salmoning home.

Friday
Last day of camp so I think to amble off alone to get some height above the west lakes. I get up on a ridge above the milky glacial lake. Perfect blue summer sky today. But then I get hooked into or on to what looks like an easy ridge to make. Keep climbing and each next ridge seems an okay way up. Gradually it becomes a cling. The rotten rock leans out and back. Near the top I have some difficulty in a chimney and remember that time long ago in the Lardeau when I couldn't go down and couldn't go back up. When I finally reach the summit it's mostly a worry about getting back down – too much adrenalin to eat lunch. But a different chute opens up to me on the way back down and delivers me onto a safe-enough ledge where I breathe a little, sigh at last.

So fear alone pummels itself inward to itself and
    becomes a fossil of another life

a piece of elk shit that lives siliconed rock-hard
    under geomorphic seabeds

a limestone sinkhole in the dark caverns of our
    falling stomachs

an unnameable saxifrage that cracks and breaks the
    rock face

the little avalanche of boulders that crackle out
    onto sheets of muddy ice and snow

the rotten Rockies rock that crumbles in the
    middle of a footstep or handhold

red-algaed snow patch too steep and icy to use

razor edge of ice and the hidden gap under the feet

this black schist or flint in the grey limestone

that's where that fear is

held there for you

alone

alive.

ULURU UTANIKI

to Jenefer

Friday, July 28/90
Today is Jenefer's birthday tomorrow on the other side of the Date Line. The plate tectonics fold ocean's time lap here, shore to shore – she'll be driving into the heat, away from the coast, through the Okanagan desert and into the mountains and into old umbilical remnant Kootenay Lake. Time. For a dip.

Low roar of sea-surf shakuhachi under
echo

Dull thud of chi-stone
cool in the macrowave

white noise and no coral underbrush
resonant hint in sync but wide

We walk clockwise around Ayers Rock this morning. The trail is quiet, clear of the crowds who ant up and down to the top. North now. We pass Kantju Gorge, full of a tour-bus-full hurrying in and out. Leave it alone.

A little chill in the lee
sun-edged shadow slit strung

her walk is all her own bones
held

Love O distant love
winter gum leaves Pacific in the sand

Inside stooped under torped overhang we scan the paintings overhead. This is a gate to place. Stop. The paint travels direct dot act. Swirl of salt wash turbined rock moves into further implants. We are in our walking shoes today.

There's that white leaf
mala puta pouch of the female hare-wallaby

how earth sits
those fellas sit

silt of the river stilled stories posed
reposed

Just before we come around the corner into the sun there's a women's sacred site fenced off. Silence and the sacred. Secret. East now and a bit of breeze. Male site escarped on corner base.

Pocked mouth shut
door to the wiltja (house) shut

Park ranger signpost words
the line of knowing on the face

far-looking rock in desinence
d-sign polarized to Cancer?

The northwest corner of the rock is a cleft slit through sandstone sun-glint henge-like horologe. We've seen the score from the start and it leads us – led with the eye through light. Unseeable distance. Blind. Aperture. Daytime night blade.

Gap to blink bridge
Gondwanaland

or the eye of silent estimation
makes another mesa-connection

kidney carried
pearl stone

Such a screen of silence on the face of the rock. The stories are there, that's obvious, but they aren't telling. A light wind as we come into the sun. A quiet wind. A fence keeps us distant from the large sacred site of fallen boulders along the north edge.

Tongue-tied track of memory
red-etched glyph

typos scarred with old info
can't decrypt these chips of the "hole" story

– now to architect the dream eme
take rope, take water

We finally work through the trees and awesome mountain images above to Mutitjulu, the one story, home of Wanampi the water snake.

Here Kuniya ritually drops sand to help control the forces of anger. There are the spears.

Dogma of extension focuses on the outskirts
nomadology hums to itself (walking along)

silence
always a field of secret legwork

mindfulness dances the polarity. Measure
no number

DEAD IN MY TRACKS: WILDCAT CREEK UTANIKI

Saturday, July 29/89
O golden, Golden morning!

West of Golden we leave the Trans-Canada and drive north about 60 km up Blaeberry River past Doubt Hill. From the chopper site we can see south to Howse Pass, a long sweep of valley brilliant in a pillowed midsummer heat-haze. An hour's spent wrapping the cars and trucks in chicken wire (old paranoid alpine parking-lot visions of the imaginary porker chewing our tires and rad hoses). Camp's just west, a ten-minute Bézier curve, swirl, and plop up Wildcat Creek, on a west slope facing east to the continental divide ridgeline of the B.C.-Alberta boundary.

Ringed by glaciers as usual
Ayesha, Baker, Parapet.

While we set up camp during the afternoon I'm in a global mode, you know, the simultaneity of the world going on right now. Paris, Kyoto, Beijing. The pavement of Tiananmen Square, the hotlines sniffing out the dissidents, CBC bulletin even email media drama of the last two months still in the air even up here, radioless, only antennaed in my bones (our name is bones, and your name is my name).

My Borders Are Altitude

and silent

                                        a paw print's cosine
climate   from the lake to the treeline
                all crumbly underfoot at the edges
                cruddy summer snowmelt
soft wet twig and bough-sprung alpine fir
                                                        but more than this
height   is my pepper
(China
          don't)
                        Now

(broken breaths contour intervals at the next hundred feet and then the sky-remembered night on the plateau above the Saskatchewan Qu'Appelle O stars what solitude your blue line and flight or weight the inverse holds me shoulder-to-shoulder my clouds as alpine meadows Newton would have cut yet minds find bandwidth in this topos-parabola chaos around the earth house

Here's this
stone under heathered turf
back bent as I dig and ruffle sacrum
drawn to the music
a slow and daily pelvic tilt of elevation
is this numbered boundary nowhere. I'm
close to 7,000 here, maybe I'll just do the horse
not to hold the world
just touch, complete
the circuit
borders such thin thoughts (apples of our eyes)
selvage yesterday's Tiananmen
a power-line buzz above, along my spine, my legs
go up and down
heart all summer-heavy
with the people

Sunday, July 30
We hike east across the valley toward Mistaya Mountain, as far as a scree slope on the south side of a granodiorite carbuncle so massive we're left only to pick and chip below the heel of.

Each rock vectors through the eyes to the height of the stomach and stops me, dazzles, dead in my tracks. Such singular surfaces are impossible to avoid. Eyes tumble, click, stop and stare, stop, stare at pink molten sunset rivers of limestone, sawtooth schist embedded.

But at this rate the hike's all history, Pleistocene.

No animals, no print, no scat. (Goat tracks? Too faint now to be sure.)

No sky-mirrored glacial swimming holes today.

No fresh water. Heather very dry. The bees buzz. Butterflies.

Doze in the sun at the bottom of a scree slope waiting for the others.

sugar of their struggle death
in China's humid night so far away
maybe that's the simplest equation
for the headwaters
television's human river
and now the sun decreases
the friction. The fingers
of my right hand trace
a band of quartz. My eyes sink
under the brim
far away
but not so far away.

Monday, the 31st

Today we climb the same side of the valley as yesterday. But now we've taken a keep-more-to-the-left route to a neck or col between Alberta and B.C., under Mistaya. Lunch beside a snow-patch lake.

when deconstruing rock
hold back the crude and the harsh
or take "reality" for simple target
the sun
                    a nation as large as China
is just another scheme for thirst and war
another centred project tunnelling earth
                    (my father's fingers poked wet into the mud of
                                        a rice paddy

rumours, the same large-spun sky here
in the thin air and during the long winter
quartz grows with the sparkle of a bridge
every stone on this mountain clicks
some old biotic tumbler locked
unlocked sadness
    not of the hundred-blossomed mountain
    not of the nine-millennia incense
    but of the dragon-slit tongue silenced
    youth before old age

After-lunch drowsiness sets in under the warmth of the sun; no birds sing; not so far away the glacier rivers roar in the July heat.

shale shard weep shard shale weep shale weep shard
shale weep shale weep shard shard weep shale shard
weep shale weep weep
shhh

Those rocks this morning on the way up appeared full of signs and messages. So I walked around in a meander and kind of grilled each striated spot for information, news of the conglomerate earth.

or
ee
ent

The others' words around me buzz and fall like horseflies. Alberta looks busy from this side: Jasper/Banff another of those new equations to satisfy war's glacial thirst. Ice-blue skyline jet-tracked.

ent
re. Pren
eur. Prende

The wooden handle of an ice axe stuck in the snow: "When making an ax handle," the pattern is occasionally too far off. Somewhere else. Out of sight, *man*. Out of mind.

snow pond fed by two large
drifts vectored off of moraine.
no real fish.
the Beijing hotline surfaces as jet-track reminder
through the high blue air
then sinks at news of the killings.
deep, like a floating thermostat.
deep, like a disappearing hook.
baited.

Tuesday, August 1
I didn't sleep very well last night because I had to get up as breakfast helper this morning – fretted about the alarm on my wristwatch being loud enough and so now mid-afternoon, sit on a slope above what we've come to call "crystal gardens" on the cool (windy) side of a grassy knoll, tired and lulled by the rush of waterfall across the valley and above this alleyway that led us here full of crystals dangled and hidden for years we poke under little rock ledges.

Quiet here. Light breeze to keep the horseflies down. I glass across a valley to a slope, for yesterday's tracks, but they've melted out. Pan back to a blurry knoll of purple yellow red pink and white on green with songs ("I don't want a sickle") I can't get out of my head and there're the others, after-lunch sprawl on the heather, Pauline reading in her flower book.

smoke in the wind, the forest below
porcupine under the wire quietly chewing our tires
is that it
smoke in the city,
slow sweep sweep of a broom in the square

Small thunderstorm coming around Trapper Peak should force us down the hill, while on this beared-over gopher-searching mountainside I linger, stopped, can't keep my eyes off the rocks and surfaces surging to not so much arrest myself in all this "otherness" as greedily scour the dripping quartz for crystal jewels for my daughters. Something lucky, something old. Something eight-spot rooted in rock, fatherness ancestral distance cut.

Hand-held Pictostone

from above Wildcat rockscape of old Renaissance bullet hole or navel with tracks going out the sides a type of Malthusian linear function along the aisles of a Saturday afternoon matinee forever pocked with edge and gouged embedded pebble from distant beach a cracked and weathered map of textured tilt propeller hummed out from omphalic sedimentary lint enough to tell story's history warped high enough in the diurnal headlines from Beijing and Shanghai so that a geologist imagining fake fish in a fake lake scrapes around the edges for shrapnel but me I think in my own mittened photos of the life look out of and far away from these threads through the hole to continue the prospect beyond impact of landing very hard and fast and past the anima button.

New moon tonight.

Wednesday
A wet day. Drizzle started last night after days of heat. The snowline is about 8,500 feet this morning. Very cool all day, off and on rain and sleet, some hail. And no respite tonight so now I sit/lie in our tent at 9 p.m. still light enough to write. I've put on my toque and gloves. No thought. Just body.

A few of us walked up the valley on the other side of Wildcat Creek and crossed many feeder creeks and the glacier river at the head of the valley. I had to take off my pants and boots once. The water came up to just above the knees. Memoried on and off all day crossing Toby moraine years ago with my brother and Loki and how that crossing, just below the crotch, rejuvenated bruised ligaments. This time my feet remain ice all day.

All these rocks. Constant mirror and presence in my eyes. More rocks than grains of sand in the whole world, I bet someone. Intricate pattern, surface, keeps stopping boot in pitch for eye to zoom. Sometimes I stop and try translating the imago-grammatic surfaces. What do I look for? This I-Chinging the earth for some other Gate of Heavenly Peace. Monotone loudspeaker in the square signalling "Go home and save your life." Old, embedded said-again family bone names?

Scale of shale
jamb stone, lintel, henge.

When the door's open
there's nothing to catch the eye.

Except the sun (blink). Now this tent
on the outside of a non-scaled phenomenon.

We'll see, Fred says to himself, the tree
as much a cinnabar flag as

– the mountains folded and folded.
"with uncountable broken arms and legs floating…"

This sky of clouds, new grass, melon
summer fields creased.

By forcing them into the centre of the square
the indelible occupies the heart until next time.

These "basins of attraction"
these grains, these fractal editions.

Night swoops very low
just a reminder.

Thursday, August 3/89
This morning I sit in the tent writing and try to situate the play in this place. The world today feels all stage. Nothing moves. A set set. There are the huge mist hackles clinging to the mountains, but no history.

Far, far down the valley a chainsaw whines.
At night now some of the creeks disappear.
Winter.

Friday, August 4/89
This last day we hike up to the col between Peyto and Mistaya but get caught in a cold mist/fog. Just behind the gauze the oval of the sun teases. The cover didn't break so we don't go further than the snowfield. We spend the rest of the day circumnavigating the head of the valley and several glacial lips up and down and home and that's eight and a half hours to a spaghetti dinner and the sky lifting to a blue evening.

Now nearly nine o'clock and the mosquitoes, after days of rain, are up for it.

Out of the corner of my eye more rocks. And out an ear I hear a few birds sing their particular song, not solitary: the creeks rush and gurgle down to the valley below. In a corner of my mind is tomorrow's two-and-a-half-hour hike out to the trailhead and then the long drive home. But nowhere else.

clear stingin' peaks
rock green moss
campion
all surface news
inked
to the bloated stone heroes
massed alongside Mao's mausoleum
same shards here
within the square
a "percolation
network"
five lines,
five soldiers a line
duende stone
thano-stone

How to Keep Digging

Fred Wah Selected Bibliography

Compiled by Ryan Fitzpatrick, Deanna Fong, and Janey Dodd from Susan Rudy's annotated bibliography *"Loose Change": Fred Wah, A Life in Writing*

> *These poems hum, deep down in that solitary interface where words take the place of place, where we sift through the archives of the self. Face the music. Save it.*
>
> —FRED WAH
> *Faking It: Poetics and Hybridity*

This selected bibliography comes out of our work compiling the Fred Wah Digital Archive (fredwah.ca). Our selections roughly follow *Scree*'s temporal frame from the early 1960s to 1991. We've included Fred's publications up to and including 1991, but have also, when looking at both the ways this work has been anthologized and discussed, included material published after this date when it shed light on Fred's earlier work.

For additional secondary materials related to Fred Wah's poetry titles published between 1962 and 1991, refer to works cited in the "Reader's Manual" by Jeff Derksen.

Books and Pamphlets

Lardeau. Toronto: Island, 1965.

Mountain. Buffalo, NY: Audit/East-West, 1967.

Among. Toronto: Coach House, 1972.

Tree. Vancouver: Vancouver Community, 1972.

Earth. Canton, NY: Institute of Further Studies, 1974.

Pictograms from the Interior of B.C. Vancouver: Talonbooks, 1975.

Loki Is Buried at Smoky Creek: Selected Poems. Vancouver: Talonbooks, 1980.

Breathin' My Name with a Sigh. Vancouver: Talonbooks, 1981.

Owners Manual. Lantzville, BC: Island Writing Series, 1981.

Grasp the Sparrow's Tail. Kyoto: Nagata Bunshodo, 1982.

Waiting for Saskatchewan. Winnipeg: Turnstone, 1985.

Music at the Heart of Thinking. Red Deer, AB: Red Deer College Press, 1987.

Rooftops. Nobleboro, ME: Blackberry Books, 1987, and Red Deer, AB: Red Deer College Press, 1988.

Limestone Lakes Utaniki. Red Deer, AB: Red Deer College Press, 1989.

So Far. Vancouver: Talonbooks, 1991.

Books and Issues (Edited or Co-Edited)

Place, Anyplace: An Anthology of Photographs and Writing from the Kootenays. Castlegar: Cotinneh, 1973.

Marlatt, Daphne. *Net Work: Selected Writing of Daphne Marlatt*. Edited by Fred Wah. Vancouver: Talonbooks, 1980.

(with Frank Davey). *The Swift Current Anthology*. Toronto: Coach House, 1986.

(with Ashok Mathur). *Oral Anthology: Interventing the Text 1991*. Calgary: self-published, 1991.

(with Susan Rudy Dorscht and Ashok Mathur). *Interventing the Text: The Calgary Conference, May 1991*. Spec. issue of *Open Letter* 8.5–6 (1993).

Journals (Edited or Co-Edited)

Tish: A Poetry Newsletter (Vancouver). 1961–1963.

Sum (Albuquerque and Buffalo). 1963–1965.

Niagara Frontier Review (Buffalo). 1964–1966.

Magazine of Further Studies (Buffalo). 1966–1968.

Scree (South Slocan). 1971–1972.

Swift Current (online). 1984–1990.

Anthologies (Included in)

Fowler, R.A., and J.K. Krueger, eds. *Free Poems Among Friends*. Castlegar, BC: Selkirk Free College Press, n.d.

Souster, Raymond, ed. *New Wave Canada*. Toronto: Contact, 1966.

Zimmerman, Daniel, ed. *The Western Gate*. Buffalo, NY: 1970.

McLeod, Gladys, ed. *Hamill's Last Stand*. Castlegar, BC: Cotinneh, 1972.

bissett, bill, ed. *End of the World Speshul Anthology*. Vancouver: blewointment, 1977.

Candelaria, Fred, ed. *New West Coast: 72 Contemporary British Columbia Poets*. Vancouver: Intermedia, 1977.

Ellis, Patricia, ed. *Western Windows: A Comparative Anthology of Poetry in British Columbia*. Vancouver: CommCept, 1977.

Page, P.K., ed. *To Say the Least: Canadian Poets from A to Z*. Toronto: Porcepic, 1979.

Bowering, George, ed. *The Contemporary Canadian Poem Anthology,* vol. 4. Toronto: Coach House, 1983.

Dyck, E.F., ed. *Essays on Saskatchewan Writing*. Regina: Saskatchewan Writers' Guild, 1986.

Newman, Shirley, and Smaro Kamboureli, eds. *Amazing Space: Writing Canadian Women Writing*. Edmonton: NeWest, 1986.

Brown, Russell, Donna Bennett, and Nathalie Cooke, eds. *An Anthology of Canadian Literature in English*. Revised and abridged edition. Toronto: Oxford University Press, 1990.

Hancock, G., ed. *Singularities, Fragments, Parafictions, Prose Poems – New Directions in Fiction and Physics*. Windsor: Black Moss, 1990.

Svendsen, Linda, ed. *Words We Call Home: Celebrating Creative Writing at UBC*. Vancouver: UBC Press, 1990.

Van Herk, Aritha, ed. *Alberta Rebound*. Edmonton: NeWest, 1990.

Andrews, Craig, and Calvin Wharton, eds. *The First 25 Years: An Anthology: Selkirk College*. Castlegar, BC: Selkirk College, 1991.

Barbour, Douglas, ed. *Beyond Tish*. Edmonton: NeWest, 1991.

Lee, Bennett, and Jim Wong-Chu, eds. *Many Mouthed Birds: Contemporary Writing by Chinese Canadians*. Vancouver: Douglas & McIntyre, 1991.

Thesen, Sharon, ed. *The New Long Poem Anthology*. Toronto: Coach House, 1991.

Hryniuk, Stella, ed. *20 Years of Multiculturalism: Successes and Failures*. Winnipeg: Saint John's College Press, 1992.

Barry, James, ed. *Coast to Coast: Canadian Stories, Poetry, Non-Fiction, and Drama*. Nelson, BC: International Thomson, 1995.

Burney, Shehla, ed. *Coming to Gum San: The Story of Chinese Canadians*. Toronto: DC Heath, 1995.

Lew, Walter, ed. *Premonitions: The Kaya Anthology of New Asian North American Poetry*. New York: Kaya, 1995.

Ramraj, Victor, ed. *Concert of Voices: An Anthology of World Writing in English*. Peterborough, ON: Broadview, 1995.

Chang, Juliana, ed. *Quiet Fire: A Historical Anthology of Asian American Poetry 1892–1970*. New York: Asian American Writers Workshop, 1996.

Kamboureli, Smaro, ed. *Making a Difference: Canadian Multicultural Literature*. Toronto: Oxford University Press, 1996.

Kudchedkar, Shirin, and Jameela Begum A., eds. *Canadian Voices*. Delhi: Pencraft, 1996.

Besner, Neil, Deborah Schnitzer, and Alden Turner, eds. *Uncommon Wealth: An Anthology of Poetry in English*. Toronto: Oxford University Press, 1997.

Banting, Pamela, ed. *Fresh Tracks: Writing the Western Landscape*. Victoria: Polestar, 1998.

Toutant, Arnold et al., eds. *Identities 9: Endless Possibilities*. Toronto: Oxford University Press, 1998.

Geddes, Gary, ed. *15 Canadian Poets ×3*. 4th ed. Toronto: Oxford University Press, 2001.

Thesen, Sharon, ed. *The New Long Poem Anthology*. 2nd ed. Vancouver: Talonbooks, 2001.

Wayman, Tom, ed. *The Dominion of Love: An Anthology of Canadian Love Poems*. Madeira Park, BC: Harbour, 2001.

Queyras, Sina, ed. *Open Field: Contemporary Canadian Poets.* New York: Persea, 2005.

Farr, Roger. *Open Text: Canadian Poetics in the 21st Century*. North Vancouver: CUE, 2009.

Grenville, Bruce, and Scott Steedman, eds. *Visions of British Columbia: A Landscape Manual*. Vancouver: Vancouver Art Gallery, 2009.

Holmes, Nancy, ed. *Open Wide a Wilderness: Canadian Nature Poems*. Waterloo, ON: Wilfrid Laurier University Press, 2009.

Bennett, Donna and Russell Brown, eds. *An Anthology of Canadian Literature*. 3rd ed. Toronto: Oxford University Press, 2010.

Interviews

Nichol, bp. "A Conversation with Fred Wah. T.R.G. Report One: Translation (Part 3)." *Open Letter* 3.9 (1978): 34–52.

Baxter, Meaghan, Jeff Derksen, and Angela Hryniuk. "An Interview with Fred Wah." *Writing* 9 (1984): 44–49.

Goddard, John "Interview with Fred Wah." *Books in Canada* (October 1986): 40–41.

Tostevin, Lola Lemire "Don't Sit Around Language: An Interview with Fred Wah." *Poetry Canada Review* 9:1 (1987): 3–5.

Tostevin, Lola Lemire " 'Music. Heart. Thinking': An Interview with Fred Wah." *Line* 12 (1988): 42–56.

Berube R.L. "One Word Generates The Next: an Interview with Fred Wah." *Skylines* (1991): 12–15.

Wah, Fred, Mireille Perron, Amy Gogarty, David Garneau, Lorne Falk, and Rob Milthorp. "Artists Writing Artists." *Open Letter* 8.5/6 (1993): 19–34.

Mathur, Ashok. "An Interview with Fred Wah on *Diamond Grill.*" *Filling Station* 10 (1997): 28–31.

Darbyshire, Peter. "Fred Wah: To Write Is to Move." *Write* 1.3 (2000): 15–16.

Fee, Margery and Sneja Gunew. "An Interview with Fred Wah." *Canadian Literature.* Canadian Literature website, 2000.

Rudy, Susan. "Fred Wah on Hybridity and Asianicity in Canada." In *Poets Talk: Conversations with Robert Kroetsch, Daphne Marlatt, Erin Mouré, Dionne Brand, Marie Annharte Baker, and Fred Wah*, edited by Pauline Butling and Susan Rudy, 143–69. Edmonton: University of Alberta Press, 2005.

Farr, Roger. " 'Surprise, Unpredictability, and Improvisation': An Interview with Fred Wah." *Capilano Review* 2.48 (2006): 5–25.

Wah, Fred, and Brian Kim Stefans. "PhillyTalks #7: Brian Kim Stefans and Fred Wah." *Jacket 2*. Jacket2 website, 2013. July 1, 2015.

Secondary Materials

Bowering, George. "Lines on the Grid." *Open Letter* 2.8 (1974): 94–99.

Tallman, Warren. "Wonder Merchants: Modernist Poetry in Vancouver During the 1960s." *Boundary 2* 3.1 (1974): 57–90.

Barbour, D. "Canadian Poetry Chronicle: III." *Dalhousie Review* 56 (1976): 560–73.

Gervais, C.H., ed. *The Writing Life: Historical & Critical Views of the Tish Movement.* Coatsworth, ON: Black Moss, 1976.

Kambourelli, Smaro. "Fred Wah, A Poetry of Dialogue." *Line* 4 (1982): 44–62.

Banting, Pamela. "Fred Wah: poet as theor(h)et(or)ician" *Open Letter* 6.7 (1987): 5–20.

Banting, Pamela. "Fred Wah's Syntax: A Geneology, A Translation." *Sagetrieb* 7.1 (1988): 99–113.

Banting, Pamela. "The Undersigned: Ethnicity and Signature Effects in Fred Wah's Poetry." *West Coast Line* 2 (1990): 83–94.

Derksen, Jeff. "Torquing Time." In *Beyond Tish,* edited by Douglas Barbour, 161–65. Edmonton: NeWest, 1991.

Dyck, Ed. "Rhetoric and Poetry and Fred Wah." In *Beyond Tish,* edited by Douglas Barbour, 194–202. Edmonton: NeWest, 1991.

Dorscht, Susan Rudy. " 'mother/father things I am also': Fred (,) Wah, Breathin' His Name with a Sigh." In *Inside the Poem: Essays and Poems in Honour of Donald* Stephens, edited by W.H. New, 216–24. Toronto: Oxford University Press, 1992.

Banting, Pamela. *Body Inc.: a theory of translation poetics.* Winnipeg: Turnstone, 1995.

Diehl-Jones, Charlene. "Fred Wah." In *Canadian Writers and Their Works,* Poetry Series 12, edited by Robert Lecker, Jack David, and Ellen Quigley, 345–434. Oakville, ON: ECW, 1996.

Diehl-Jones, Charlene. "Fred Wah and the Radical Long Poem." In *Bolder Flights: Essays on the Canadian Long Poem,* edited by Frank M. Tierney and Angela Robbeson, 139–49. Ottawa: University of Ottawa Press, 1998.

Garrett-Petts, William F., and Donald Lawrence. *Photographic Encounters: The Edges and Edginess of Reading Prose Pictures and Visual Fictions.* Edmonton: University of Alberta Press, 2000.

Stefans, Brian Kim. "Remote Parsee: An Alternative Grammar of Asian North American Poetry." In *Telling It Slant: Avant-Garde Poetics of the 1990s*, edited by Mark Wallace and Steven Marks, 43–75. Tuscaloosa: University of Alabama Press, 2001.

Boughn, Michael. "Olson's Buffalo." In *The World in Time and Space: Towards a History of Innovative American Poetry in Our Time*, edited by Edward Foster and Joseph Donahue. Jersey City, NJ: Talisman, 2003.

Budde, Robert. "After Postcolonialism: Migrant Lines and the Politics of Form in Fred Wah, M. Nourbese Philip, and Roy Miki." In *Is Canada Postcolonial? Unsettling Canadian Literature*, edited by Laura Moss, 282–94. Waterloo, ON: Wilfrid Laurier University Press, 2003.

Gunew, Sneja. "Somatic Belonging in Public Spheres." In *Die Lektüre der Welt: Zur Theorie, Geschichte und Soziologie kultureller Praxis/Worlds of Reading: On the Theory, History, and Sociology of Cultural Practice*, edited by Helmut Heinze and Christiane Weller, 297–304. Frankfurt: Peter Lang, 2004.

Day, Iyko. "Interventing Innocence: Race, 'Resistance,' and the Asian North American Avant-Garde." In *Literary Gestures: The Aesthetic in Asian American Writing*, edited by Rocio G. Davis and Sue-Im Lee, 35–52. Philadelphia: Temple University Press, 2006.

Hart, Jonathan. "Some Reflections on Asian-Canadian Poetry and Culture: Fred Wah, Joy Kogawa, Roy Miki, and Others." *Canadian Review of Comparative Literature* 36.3 (2009): 310–20.

Miki, Roy. "The Poetics of the Hyphen: Fred Wah, Or the Ethics of Reading 'Asian Canadian' Writing." In *Virtually American? Denationalizing North American Studies*, 111–22. Heidelberg, Germany: Universitätsverlag Winter, 2009.

Helms, Gabriele. "Contemporary Canadian Poetry from the Edge: An Exploration of Literary Ecocriticism." In *Greening the Maple: Canadian Ecocriticism in Context*, edited by Ella Soper and Nicholas Bradley, 145–65. Calgary: University of Calgary Press, 2013.

Redling, Erik. " 'When I Tree Myself': Paratextual Elements in Fred Wah's Poetic Life Writings." In *Ecology and Life Writing*, edited by Alfred Hornung and Baisheng Zhao, 241–55. Heidelberg, Germany: Universitätsverlag Winter, 2013.

Fickle, Tara. "English Before Engrish: Asian American Poetry's Unruly Tongue." *Comparative Literature Studies* 51.1 (2014): 78–105.

Web Resources

Red Log (fredwah.org): Fred's personal blog.

The Fred Wah Digital Archive (fredwah.ca): bibliography and repository of works.

Parliamentary Poet YouTube (youtube.com): Videos made by Fred when Poet Laureate.

Slought Foundation (slought.org): Recordings made by Fred at the 1963 Vancouver Poetry Conference.

PennSound (writing.upenn.edu/pennsound): Various video and audio recordings of Fred.

Kootenay School of Writing (kswnet.org/index.cfm): Book launch for *So Far* (October 26, 1991).

Permissions

Cover image, *Envelope Sketch* (1967) by Takao Tanabe, reproduced with permission of the artist and Simon Fraser University Galleries.

Digital scans of *Tree* and *Earth* courtesy the Fred Wah Digital Archive.

Illustrations in *Tree* by Lauren "Bird" Hamilton reproduced with permission of the artist.

Illustrations in *Pictographs from the Interior of British Columbia* by John Corner reproduced with permission of the Estate of John Corner.

"Elite" and "This Dendrite Map: Father/Mother Haibun" from *Waiting for Saskatchewan* reproduced with permission of Turnstone Press, Winnipeg.

Index of Titles and First Lines

Untitled poems are listed only by first line. End-of-line punctuation in each first line is retained as it appears in the original poem; ellipses indicate the continuing line of a prose poem.

In poems with numbered parts, only the first line of the first part is included.

G

H

I